Bestiality of the Involved

Also by Spring Ulmer

The Age of Virtual Reproduction
Benjamin's Spectacles

Bestiality of the Involved is a narrative tapestry woven of memoir and metaphor. I've rarely encountered any work so intensely personal that wasn't, on some level, either boastful, intimate to the point of exhibitionism, or making a plaintive case for victimhood. You'll find none of those flaws here—this is a woman at a certain point in her life who quietly opens her door and her mind to a reader and says, "Come in, this is who I am, this is how I think." At times her honesty is such that a reader feels he's trespassing, but her verbal precision and exceptional powers of observation keep drawing him deeper into her stories and her commitments. Ulmer is a writer who never shrinks from the responsibilities of the individual conscience, and there is much here that will compel the reader to examine his own. I was reminded of one reviewer's first encounter with W.G. Sebald, whose external/internal journeys amount to so much more than travel books. "If I ever find myself on an interminable journey," the reviewer wrote, "this is the one seatmate whose conversation would make every mile worthwhile."

—Hal Crowther, *An Infuriating American*

In *Bestiality of the Involved*, Ulmer shows how to search the self for traces of a broader intelligence, and offer, in response, an unrestrained, generous pathos. Out of the sheer range of her travels and encounters, she has produced a book that affirms what it is to be humane, involved, and capable of containing stories. There is an ancient connection between place and feeling, affect and landscape, and in Ulmer's book, I discovered it anew.

—Emmanuel Iduma, *A Stranger's Pose*

This book is as erudite as it is empathetic. Ultimately about the yearning for a child, *Bestiality of the Involved* is also about torture, terrorism, citizenship, and art. Ulmer cites a medley of influences here, but two that stand out are John Berger and Susan Sontag. Like Berger, Ulmer looks closely at the world, and like Sontag, she refuses to look away when what the world gives back is not beautiful, but hideous, heartbreaking, or cruel. This book is a must read for anyone committed to participating fully and humanely in this savage life.

—Sarah Viren, *Mine*

Spring Ulmer writes a pure prose, out of the blue, undiluted, shooting straight, easily revelatory. She roams left to write in English but her gaze is sideways and panopticon— from Adorno and Courbet to Goya and then you're hooked to find out who and what else. *Bestiality of the Involved* is a renegade text, as I call my own rare collection of cherished books that were written from the trenches of life and liberty. You keep turning the pages and you keep wondering who is she talking to? There is something scarily Kafkaesque about the uncanny moment when you realize she has been writing just for you.

—Hamid Dabashi, *Europe and its Shadows*

Bestiality of the Involved

Spring Ulmer

Etruscan Press

Etruscan Press
Wilkes University
84 West South Street
Wilkes-Barre, PA 18766
(570) 408-4546

 Wilkes
University

www.etruscanpress.org

Published 2020 by Etruscan Press
Printed in the United States of America
Cover design by Lisa Reynolds
Interior design and typesetting by Todd Espenshade
The text of this book is set in Minion Pro.

First Edition

17 18 19 20 5 4 3 2 1

Library of Congress Cataloguing-in-Publication Data

Names: Ulmer, Spring, author.
Title: Bestiality of the Involved / Spring Ulmer.
Description: First edition. | Wilkes-Barre : Etruscan Press, 2020.
Identifiers: LCCN 2019033504 (print) | LCCN 2019033505 (ebook) |
    ISBN 9781733674126 (trade paperback) | ISBN 9781733674133 (ebook)
Classification: LCC PS3621.L49 A6 2020 (print) | LCC PS3621.L49
    (ebook) | DDC 814/.6--dc23
LC record available at https://lccn.loc.gov/2019033504
LC ebook record available at https://lccn.loc.gov/2019033505

Please turn to the back of this book for a list of the sustaining funders of Etruscan Press.

This book is printed on recycled, acid-free paper.

For André

...a choice between the involuntary ataraxy—an esthetic life due to weakness—and the bestiality of the involved. Both are wrong ways of living... The guilt of a life which purely as a fact will strangle other life...is irreconcilable with living.

—Theodor Adorno

CONTENTS

Bestiality of the Involved

A Short History of the
Distance Between Art and Life

Archways perfectly frame the dead. Of a man's castration, all we see is the sword blade. An old woman poised, knife out, to attack a fur-capped rapist signifies not only the unending nature of violence but changes the emphasis from what is being shown to the fact that it is being shown *again*. Susan Sontag argues that Francesco Goya did not sexualize his subjects. He presented them, she insists, 'thickly clothed.' What desexualizes Goya's subjects has to do, Sontag claims, with the way Goya's naked dead recline, their nakedness out of reach, mythologized. Unlike Goya, a pornographic renderer focuses on body parts not composition, does not reference any historical moment, and is only concerned with the titillating *now*. Goya was immune to now; he was always anticipating *again*. Goya's presentation of suffering is both mythic and real—a real allegory, Gustave Courbet would say.

'It is rare to meet the most complete expression of poverty,' Courbet wrote in a letter about the subjects that would become immortalized in his 1849 painting *The Stonebreakers*. He described in this letter the look of the older man: 'sunburned, wearing worn clothes, old sabots, one leather suspender holding up his trousers,' and concluded: 'Alas, in these circumstances, one begins like this, ends the same way.'

It used to be that I often came across my father on his knee in the same pose the old man takes in Courbet's *The Stonebreakers*. Courbet was born among stonebreakers; he, John Berger argues, painted representations of rocks the same way he painted portraits. I learned to paint by mixing pigment into my father's cement, pinking it to bring out the rose color in the stone, and later I learned to fit words together as I searched for perfectly fitting rocks to fill the gaps in the walls my father built. Stones are silent, ancient. My father split them from the earth with plug and feather, and wrestled them into walls. He worked his own hours, quitting when the weather turned too cold for the mortar to properly harden. In his old age,

he moves stones from the field in front of our house to the gulley near the
road, freeing the soil so that more ever-blooming lilac roots might take
hold.

The other day, walking in the forest near Montpelier, Vermont, not far from
where I was reared, a stranger stopped me. He asked whether I had seen
any hunters on the trail. I told him that I had. He began to talk, massaging
what appeared to be improbably stiff fingers on one of his gloved hands.
He spoke of the trails he had walked in his day, the bear cubs he had seen
boxing like kangaroos. He described how to get to remote locations and
what kind of bridges he crossed. Then he mentioned in passing that he had
shot himself in the chest with a .45 Colt. The shrapnel, he explained, exited
his left arm. Loss of love, he said. I can talk about it now without my voice
cracking.

The stranger did not stop talking. I listened, as I do, and asked an odd
question. It was obvious that this man belonged to the hills whose trails he
described, as much as he belonged to his trauma, his hand with its bullet
wound stiff, unbending. I stood opposite him on the forested hill, sunlight
glinting off the snow, as if off the smooth face of a wristwatch angled just
so, wondering at the blinding pain this man made visible.

In Goya's *The Third of May 1808*, a Spaniard raises his hands before a French
execution squad. The light—painted as if cast by a single lantern—engulfs
him. His right upraised palm is marked—a stigmata? What does it mean to
stare down death? I think of the hunter who shot himself, crippled by the
injustice of love having turned her back, deciding against him.

My mother studied Goya. She went to Spain in her late teens just to see his
etchings then kept in the unlit Prado basement. I imagine her pulling on
white gloves, handling each print in the near dark, straining to make out
the Spanish *tampoco* at the base of Goya's most famous *dibujo* in which a
man hangs from a stump, his nightshirt long, trousers bunched around
his ankles, a soldier looking on. The young woman in white gloves is not
inconsistent with the old woman my mother has become with slivers of

hay in her hands, dirt under her nails, horseflies in her hair and biting her forearms. Her utter engagement with the world, her sense of earnestness and selflessness remain unchanged.

I envy my mother's closeness to the land, yet I am terrified of the land's power over her. I am scared by how thin she gets (her body a sketch), how brown, how dedicated to digging. I know what it is like to squat all day, planting seedlings, the sun burning my back where my shirt comes un-tucked. I know the continual arithmetic of how much labor is left, so as to know when I might seek shade, and how thankful I am to break for hot tea. My mother doesn't break; she continues working day after day. I envy her ability to tend to life so determinedly. Goya tended to his black paintings this same way.

Goya's black paintings were cut from plaster walls of *La Quinto del Sordo* and placed in the Prado after his death. By the time he had attacked the walls of his house with oil paint, he had gone deaf. He painted the wild-eyed dog, drowning in landscape, by the door.

Sontag claimed that Goya's etchings approximate suffering rather than mimic atrocities the way photos do. I am not convinced that any one mate-rial better critiques war. All critiques, no matter how carefully crafted, are rhetorical and never for a second free from interpretation. Neither cutlines nor etched lines tell us what to see. We are experts at seeing what we want; this talent—call it denial, self-deception, optimism, cunning, violence, or fantasy—looms larger than the real. We make myths of reality.

Courbet painted *The Origin of the World*, a painting of a woman's dark-haired pubis, so that we might look at the real and acknowledge just how mythic it is. We come from this place, from these people, that part of the body? Courbet renders where we come from in the most blatant manner. It is suspected that he took to bed this model whose pubis he made famous. Perhaps he painted her curly hair brown on purpose to hide her identity, or else he did so simply to heighten the scandal, for the model is thought to have been the painter James Whistler's red-haired model and lover, Joan-na Hiffernan. Whistler, however, always painted her clothed. In Whistler's

The White Girl, Hiffernan appears cloaked in a long white gown, standing atop a bear rug—the bear's head whole, fangs bared. The two painters' approaches to the same beloved subject could hardly have been more at odds.

All a painter like Courbet had to do, Whistler ranted after Courbet completed *The Origin of the World*, 'was to open his eyes and paint what was there in front of him! beautiful nature and the whole caboodle! that was all there was to it! and then people went to see it!' Once a follower of Courbet's, so thorough was Whistler's rejection of Nature after his muse betrayed him that he broke up with Hiffernan and committed himself to making art solely for art's sake. Artifice was thereby born. Hiffernan, meanwhile, complicating this fetid plot, adopted Whistler's illegitimate child born to him by his parlor maid.

Whistler grew into a quite trippy dude. Robert Hayden's poem 'The Peacock Room' takes as its focus a room decorated by Whistler that serves to shelter Hayden from the horrors of Hiroshima, Watts, and My Lai. The blank verse ultimately narrows in on Thomas Jekyll, original designer of the room who was literally driven insane by Whistler's erasure of his work. Whistler's stylized peacocks become metaphors of both horror and beauty to Hayden. 'What is art? What is life?' Hayden asks in the poem.

Hayden was made famous by Black Arts poets years after they accused him of being poet first and black second. Simon Gikandi asserts that art is one of the first places where black bodies can be recognized as human beings and modern subjects, as art always forces upon the viewer recognition of the Other. Yet, Gikandi argues, 'art has been made custodian of universal identity all the while race has become the phenomenological sign of difference.' In other words, art, one might argue, has the potential to challenge viewers to read beyond racial difference. Julius Lester, extrapolating upon Hayden's refusal to be categorized as a black poet, states that his mentor's 'desire to be regarded as nothing more or less than a poet was not a denial of his blackness, but the only way he knew of saying that blackness was not big enough to contain him.'

Hayden's art remains profoundly political because he was not interested in rhetoric. He dismissed Black Power ideology, as it reminded him, he wrote in his unpublished notes, of the pressure to conform, which the Marxists had exerted on him thirty years prior. 'I suppose the cruelty of art is that it outlasts those who make it,' Hayden confessed in an interview, adding, 'What is art anyway? Why does it mean so much that it can determine one's whole life, make a person sacrifice everything for it, even drive one mad? What is it?'

Goya once said that he would rather shoot than paint. Goya was a hunter. Courbet also loved to hunt. Goya and Courbet painted hunting dogs, and both painters rendered, at one time or another, dogs looking up at their masters for the crucial cue. The distance between this instant and what is to come after is the distance between life and death, and the distance, too, one could say, between life and art.

Realism shows us, as it mirrors our mortality, what beasts we are—all of us born from a watery grotto and reared to poise atop death, salivating, fangs bared, before we return to the cracked earth, spent, suspenders and bodices torn. Similarly, realism's freezing of the moment *right before* death occurs, or *right before* pleasure is awarded or taken away, or *right before* a being is brought into the world or taken out of it, mitigates against *again*. Yet awareness of and the ability to see and represent the mythic within the real is what can, as Goya foresaw, change the cue, enable us to see otherly and *again*, as well as help us come to understand the difference between waiting at the door and bursting through it.

A Short History of Greek Blues

Charles Knight's paintings of the striped-coated, multi-toed Dawn Horse reminded me of the way I had been awed by Arthur Evans's reconstruction of Knossos as a child. The colors of the Knossos murals had fascinated me: the rust-red of the walls, the blue and white painted waves, and bull-dancing designs. I had entered the ruins desirously, not caring what was true about the reconstruction or what was false. Of course, later I came to understand archaeologists' and scholars' horror at Evans's egomaniacal interpretation of history, his reconstructions based on a longing to substantiate Greek legends and myths, but I never lost the appreciation of what Evans showed me: how the past could be made seem alive. Knight's illustrations similarly showed me glimpses of something beyond the realm of what I could imagine—a fifty-five-million-year-old, three- and four-toed, twelve-pound, two-foot-tall horse.

I had learned of the Dawn Horse while currying a pony and wondering whether or not I had brushed its fetlock hard enough. Is this a piece of dried mud? Should I worry about not being able to brush it out? I'd asked Rachel, the stable manager at the farm on Corfu I had fled to after learning that my father was dying.

That's left over from when horses had toes. It's called a chestnut, she'd informed me. Down below is the ergot.

~

I thought horses could get me caring about life again.

I was talking to a stranger named Christos at a café in Corfu Town. I wasn't in the habit of riding on the backs of scooters with men I didn't know, so there was no reason why I had climbed onto Christos's after he waved me down along the seaside esplanade. Perhaps I got on because I was carrying a heavy bag filled with books. Perhaps I was flattered. I had been looking to be picked up in some form or other. Rather than just hurrying home from the Durrell School Library on my day off, I had straddled the stone seawall, tired of the traffic, glad for the breeze off the sea. I wanted to experience life outside the farm gates, but it was easier to read. I fished around in my bag and pulled out Yannis Ritsos's *Late into the Night*, telling myself that maybe someone might just happen by. A Marxist hope, the introduction read, had kept Ritsos alive, sustaining him through years of imprisonment and torture, but the fall of the Eastern Bloc had shattered him. Within a year of this collapse, he was dead.

I had inhaled the first poem, 'Misguided Pursuits.' The poem ended painfully: 'a window supposedly open to the miracle of the world? Who were you trying to fool? Surely not yourself. Go on then...' Then Christos had appeared on his moped and cut the engine. Where are you from? What's your name? Spring? We don't have that name in Greece. You work with ponies? How many ponies? Thirty? That's a lot of work. It's your day off? Come on; let's go for a coffee.

Christos lived off a pension he received from Olympic Airlines, and wanted, he confessed, a wife and baby to give his life meaning. After we downed our espressos, he lamented, You should have ordered a Greek coffee. I could have read your grounds.

His bringing up coffee grounds seemed like a sign. Years ago, when I was nine and bicycling 3,000 kilometers around Greece with my parents, my mother had read the dark marks of drained grounds. She had said she could see me grown up—for I had breasts—with horses. I had believed her. Christos was asking me a question. No, I wouldn't accompany him to his house for bean soup. He tried again. I shook my head. We continued to talk, the gaps in our conversation growing more and more uncomfortable. You should be worried, he said finally, if you want to have a child. With your age, soon it will be too late.

A man with slightly hunched shoulders and inset eyes, Christos wasn't tall. He had recently given up smoking, he told me, and had put on some weight. He went inside and settled the bill. I'll give you a ride to where you're staying, he said, returning to our table.

I tried to refuse. He took me first to a forest. We walked through the towering cypress trees. Purple cyclamen dotted the undergrowth. English and Greek royalty had lived on the grounds and now it was a park. The sun shone. The sea was gauzy. Christos crunched a Daphne leaf in his hand. It smelled, I thought, of burnt sweet corn. We spoke of politics (it's the same everywhere—lies) and the economy.

Christos mentioned how people he knew were getting sucked into computers, not spending time doing anything else. He told me, too, of the four million olive trees that grew on Corfu and were governmentally protected, but which scarcely anyone harvested anymore.

Giant millstones for pressing olives were propped here and there around the palace grounds. Suddenly, we stumbled—or so it seemed to me—upon the crumbling ruins of a Doric temple. We approached the stone foundation as if such ruins were common—and for Christos they were. The temple had been built in the fifth century B.C. That place in the center there, Christos said, pointing to a basin-shaped section in the middle of the temple, was for sacrifices.

We turned and walked along another path. As we approached the edge of the woods, I asked Christos how it was that he was so young and already received a pension.

I'm bipolar. My doctor tells me I'm lucky, he said and smiled. I have more of the happier side.

~

I went down to the ocean and jumped in. The water was cold at first, then warm, and the stones underfoot slick with seaweed. I didn't stay in long, but slipped out, and lay on a rock in my soaked exercise bra and ex-boyfriend's underwear, thinking, as the sea lapped at a fallen tree to my left, that I was the only person along the rocky shore. I had my eyes closed and was draped there on the rock, when I heard heavy breathing. I sat up. Two feet away, coming toward me, was a spearfish hunter still wearing his scuba mask and snorkel. The snorkel's plastic tube amplified the raspy sound of the hunter's breath. In one hand he clenched a number of small fish, and in the other he held a heavy-duty, hydraulic spear. I felt defenseless there, half-naked on the rock. His trident looked particularly sharp.

In Ritsos's poem 'Two in the Afternoon,' skin divers in their wetsuits come in from the water, carrying fins and an octopus. One looks at the narrator expectantly. Hello, the diver says. Hello, the narrator replies, feeling as if he should say more.

I felt the same way as this postmodern Poseidon approached, as if something else should have occurred, or had occurred, as he made his way past, sliding along the shore in his jelly slippers.

~

The fig tree was blowing in the wind. The rush of its leaves and limbs sounded as loud as the now crawling sea. I closed my eyes, snug in my bunk. The wind bent the elastic arms of milk-sap-heavy, thousand pound branches just beyond my window. That night I dreamed that a sea creature covered with barnacles and green algae rose from the sea and looked at me.

~

The wind blew the electric out pre-dawn. Thomas, one of the farmhands, was in the kitchen. He'd lit candles. I made our usual morning coffees on the gas stove, and slathered a piece of bread with honey and tahini. It's a shit life, Thomas said, sitting down at the table.

Why a shit life? I asked in Greek.

I just work, work, then go home, come back, work more. It's wet. There are trees down in town, up the hill.

Doesn't having kids make your life any better?

Yes, but not when they don't have jobs and are asking for money. Thomas looked beaten, his face pinched with wrinkles.

I walked out into the dark. The eucalyptus bark was slippery and the wind fierce. I still hadn't registered the force of the gale when Roben, a rescued gelding, came up from behind, and knocked me down. As I fell, the alfalfa slipped from my arms and my hands flew up to protect my head. It wasn't as bad as I'd feared, looking up at his underbelly. As soon as he turned from me to the fallen alfalfa, I picked myself up, slid down the muddy hill, and swung my body up and over the aluminum fence rail.

~

Winter neared and we started burning the muckheap. On fire, the mass of dung, mud, and soiled straw was beautiful. Of course, it reeked. Rachel and I stared at the flame. I suggested it would make a nice kiln. When I was young, my parents and I had dug a pit and filled it with ceramic ware we had fashioned by hand and burnished with the backs of spoons. We had covered the pots with sheep dung and then set the whole thing on fire. After the fire had died, the burnish beneath the black pots shone blue and blinked in the sun.

~

Penas's triptych was as red as the muckheap's caverns, and his dark flowery canvases had the same dense, murky feeling the burning heap had. A forty-four-year-old painter who lived and painted in a villa not far from the center of Corfu Town, Penas was always appearing and disappearing, bringing over elaborate pastries, and inviting himself to coffee. He reminded me of the last man I had dated, a gay, indigenous rights lawyer from Spain. I found Penas's manic nature enticing. So enticing, in fact, that after a dinner, drinks, and magical cigarettes, I was waltzing with him in his living room. The moon was full. Josephine Baker was singing. I gazed at Penas's triptych of red, red flowers. Grotesquely red. Caravaggio red. Deep, dark red.

~

The fallen pine needles after days of rain were red. I mucked around them and the sprouting wild onions in the Skyrian ponies' fields. Victor, my favorite yearling, nipped at me. His black hair furled in a spiral in the center of his forehead where I kissed him. I had to be careful not to let him bite or boss me. He was growing big. I gave his nose a little slap.

~

Shortly before Christmas, a policeman shot and killed a fifteen-year-old in Athens. For days afterward, the streets were on fire. Eventually, the chaos grew into a national strike. Greeks have always been like this, Sylvia, the ponies' owner, told me. The only time we've ever had a stable economy was when there were dictators. We have to be kept in line, told what to do. Then everything goes smoothly, works. We're a greedy people.

You'd think Greece, the birthplace of democracy—

Yes, we're the birthplace of democracy, but only during the dictatorships have we ever had any stability, Sylvia cut me off.

But no one wants to live in a dictatorship, I protested.

No, of course not.

I thought of the 30,000 Euros it cost to feed Sylvia's ponies and the money into which she had been born—her father a tobacco salesman.

I thought of Ritsos, whose poem 'Epitaphios,' about the police killing of a young tobacco-worker in the 1930s, was still sung at protests; I wanted to believe his dream, no matter what I knew about what killed him, wasn't dead.

~

The church overlooked the taunting aquamarine bay of an otherwise ominous, steel blue ocean. It was evening, the clouds heavy, and the shadows on the walls of the house across from the church gigantic. I waved at my own dark form. I could see rice whipping like a windstorm above the heads of the onlookers. I stood in the cold, fingering the unthrown bag of rice in my pocket. A girl in black fishnets had handed the bag to me. The church courtyard was pink and white tiled, the pink thoroughly faded. A Christmas light in the shape of a holiday bell glowed above my head. Olive branches grabbed at the guitarist and accordion player. I feared the musicians' fingers would soon grow too numb to serenade. I was at a wedding of someone I didn't know, wearing someone else's long black coat to cover my jeans, my scuffed shoes setting me ever further apart from Greek women in their high heels.

~

The day Rosie the pony was kicked by a fellow mare, I arrived to find her on the ground. Rachel ran to her, led her into the stable, and then, after she collapsed, asked me to hold her. I sat in the straw, stroking her mane, and offering her my knee as a pillow. She was in too much pain to keep her head in one position, and her eyes were large. Her breath came like hiccups and her entire body quivered.

A vet was summoned, painkillers given, and the hole in Rosie's side wrapped within hours. The bandage was too tight, however, or perhaps the herniated hole was incorrectly corseted, as within minutes sweat poured down Rosie's head and neck. Not long after this, Rachel removed the makeshift belt.

As soon as the sedatives kicked in, Rosie was able to stand again and even eat. But she shivered, wet with sweat. Cushing's disease had already turned her coat into a jungle of matted, half-grey, half-burnt umber curls. Due to this hormonal imbalance, no matter how much she ate, she gained no weight. The morning passed quickly. Rosie wandered, drugged, in and out of her stable. Rachel gave her another painkiller in the evening. I crept down later, in the dark of the moonless night, to check on her. The bowling-ball-sized hernia now hung out of her left side. It had turned hard and diarrhea coated her tail.

The next day, Rosie wouldn't eat anything. The only thing we could really do, it seemed, was wait. Rachel gave her another painkiller and asked me to brush her. I brushed her and then I combed her mane and spent a long time disentangling the dried shit from her tail. She stood for me, patiently, at the edge of the field attached to her stable. She stood there all day, in fact, not eating, barely wetting her lips, refusing our offers of apple and carrot slices.

The vet arrived again, and soon he was sweating. Air bubbles, he explained, had collected everywhere beneath Rosie's skin. He kept wiping his forehead with his sleeve. Her heart was strong, though, he said, removing the stethoscope from his ears. Normally he would operate. But it was senseless to, in this case, given Rosie's age and condition. If the kick had missed the spleen and she could survive on water for a few days, she might make it. The hole would heal; the bubbles also pass. But Cushing's meant she needed constant feeding. He shook his head and readied his syringe.

For the next five minutes I stroked Rosie as the vet stuck needle after needle into her neck, sucking out the air bubbles. She must have been inhaling at the time of the impact, he explained. He'd once known a cat to survive this same condition—subcutaneous emphysema. But that was a cat.

Rosie's stubborn, I told Rachel. She's got that going for her.

Rachel laughed.

I knew it wasn't a real laugh. I knew, too, that she didn't want comforting as we turned off Rosie's stable light.

~

Rachel found Rosie dead the next morning and covered her with straw. A backhoe came a day later. I grabbed at the straw pile in the stable corner. Hurriedly, Rachel and I uncovered her bloated body. Then five of us hauled her out of the stable and across the pebbled earth, to the backhoe's gaping trough-like mouth. Even with her body so bloated, her curls looked the same. Like a child's beloved bear, I thought, trying not to think of anything else, as the backhoe turned with her in its mouth and headed up the hill.

The earth at the top of the hill was pure sand, even five feet down. The backhoe's back claw kept dredging up dry soil. Eight months had passed without a real rain. It was a wonder there was any water left on the island. I stood under a tree's red fall leaves. The backhoe operator was talking on his cell phone as he swiveled Rosie toward the hole. Her body thudded against the dry dirt. Rachel climbed into the hole with her. After turning Rosie's head to the side in a more peaceful position, Rachel stepped up onto Rosie's hip, and reached out a hand.

~

I pulled on some clothes, packed my shoulder bag with books, and headed off to town on foot, passing the hotel district with its gaudy new buildings decorated in bright pastel colors. I reached the ruins of the sixth century B.C. shipyards and the bombed church of Ayia Kerkyra at exactly the same time as the morning sun. The white stone boat of the building glowed in the field. I took the side road heading north past the old deserted thread factory surrounded by a concrete wall slathered with colorful graffiti, and made my way through Garitza, past the grocery, bakery, and lamb roasting on the sidewalk spit. It had been two weeks since my last trip to town, and I didn't register just how overwhelmed I was by the traffic, not to mention how affected I was by life at the farm, until I heard a noise in the street, turned, and out of the corner of my eye saw what I expected to be a pony. I looked again. It was just a person crossing the street.

~

Christine's face was powered, her hair silver and bobbed. She sat next to Sylvia and they and another British couple spoke of a woman they all knew who had been attacked while walking a dog. It wasn't a woman any of them liked.

Jens picked at his lamb. I didn't look his direction. I had just told him that it would have been better had he not come to visit. She cost me 800,000 pounds, Christine was saying. She was still talking about the woman who had been attacked.

Christine's voice reeked of money. It liked hearing itself talk. I tried not to listen. I picked at my vegetables, but as soon as the conversation turned to the favorite expat topic of criticizing the native population, I got up and began clearing the table. I only have two Greek friends I trust, a British guest named Andrew stated.

And one of them's Sylvia? I heard Christine ask.

One of them's Sylvia. Don't even get me started on the Corfiots. They're idiots. I don't trust a bloody one of them.

The Albanians, as a group, were the next targets. I fumed in the kitchen, stacking up plates noisily, rinsing them with the blistering hot water that ran out of the tap straight from the hot water heater. Jens came in, his hands as full as mine of dirty plates. The horror of the situation made our own bitterness less sour. He put down the plates and hugged me. I'm sorry, I said.

Me, too.

There followed a general exodus from the kitchen, as Sylvia led Christine into the living room. Jens, Christine is waiting for you in the other room. We've lit a fire, Sylvia called from the kitchen door.

Jens and I made our way to where Christine had unrolled the life-sized photo of her supposed Jackson Pollock painting that she had purchased for two dollars at an apartment sale. She set the photo on the table beside the golden-foil wrapped chocolate truffles Sylvia had been saving for the occasion. Jens, who practiced spectroscopy at Harvard, bent over the image as Christine launched into the story of how she had matched the fingerprints on the painting to those of Pollock's. I just have a feeling that this is a Pollock. There's too much attention paid to how it's been painted. And I have a knack for finding originals, Christine was saying.

Do you like that painting? Does it match your décor or something? Andrew asked. He, too, had adjourned to the living room.

Well, it did match the furniture in my apartment in New York, when I had my Tudor furniture. But now I have more Venetian style—

No, I mean, do you like that painting, or does it just match—

I think it's a brilliant painting.

I think it's crap. What's it supposed to be anyway? Andrew inquired.

It's paint, dribbled.

It was revolutionary for its time, I offered.

Pollock freed the American artist from the figure, Jens added.

Well, I don't understand it, Andrew said. It's ugly to me.

I know what you mean, I said, thinking of the conversation Jens and I had had earlier that week about painting. Jens had defended Rothko and other painters who were interested for the most part in color and light. I had stuck by Goya, arguing for social and political content.

I don't like paintings that are just one-liners, Jens had argued.

Goya's etchings are about the horrors of war, but they're also all about light, I had said. I go to them for light.

Well, I'm sorry I couldn't help you, Jens told Christine now, turning away from the photo of the painting. I do have a friend, though, who would be happy to look at the painting for you and do a material analysis.

Would he do it for free? I've already spent $8,000 on researching the painting and I can't continue to—

I'm afraid he's not inexpensive. The work we do is labor intensive, and to do it we need special equipment, folders of research, years of training.

Jens shook Christine's hand.

~

I bet Jens took it in stride, but you didn't, Rachel said when I told her about the evening.

That's exactly right.

He must be used to people like that. Must talk to them every day. I've never met such people in my life!

The stables were dreary. It was raining again. For the past year, Jens had been looking at Rothko, attempting to figure out how to preserve Harvard's collection of these fading paintings. To me, the answer seemed simple: let them fade. But Jens believed in the atmosphere Rothko had worked so hard to create. Rothko's work was all about color and light and, now that the paintings' colors were changing, it could be argued that the paintings were no longer really the works Rothko once painted. Now they meant something else. Jens thought he might correct the color of Harvard's faded Rothko's with colored projections. When he had told me this, I'd said, So now we're botoxing paintings?

Yet wasn't I the one who had been so entranced with Evans's reconstructed Knossos? Perhaps, I found myself thinking, I was coming to value art dying a dignified death.

~

Two days after Jens left, Nikos, the seventy-year-old Greek farrier, tried to kiss me in the tack room. Rachel and I had spent the morning checking the fence. We had uprooted weeds, retied the fabric fencing, but still hadn't been able to see where the current was getting waylaid. What did an artist's being freed from the figure—or the ground—really mean?

~

The mud in the fields was so deep it was unnavigable in places. Rain fell constantly and the temperature dropped. My fingers turned rough and reptile-like. My elbows ached from shoveling shit. The wet bags I slugged out of the horse's fields grazed the electric fence, sending shocks up my arms. I was replacing Ikarus's salt block with a new red ring of salt, imprinted with the letters S-I-N, when I noticed a rat crawling through the mud. It wasn't crawling fast enough. There's a dying rat in Ikarus's stable, I called over to Rachel. Ikarus won't eat it, will he?

No. You can take a shovel and hit it on the head if you want.

I didn't want to. I picked up Ikarus's black feed bucket dotted with leftover bits of brown sugar beet. I didn't feel like a coward for not killing the rat. Even if it wasn't a natural death, it was still the rat's own.

When I went back down to hay later, the rat was on its back, feet waving. Ikarus sniffed at it. I picked up a branch, thinking I could maneuver the dying rat out of the field to a place under tree cover. There, it would be less scared, I reasoned. But as soon as I stuck the stick under the fence it occurred to me that moving the rat would probably disturb it, make it suffer more. Will there be love after Duende? Jens had asked me at some point during his visit, referring to the only person I had ever thought I'd marry.

No, I'd said.

~

In the courtyard of the Monastery of Saint Theodore the Recruit and Saint George Triumphant, a monk rested on a pair of crutches. At the edge of the adjoining field, a balding man balanced on a plank of scaffolding. I watched as the man lifted boulder after boulder, trying them out in different places along the wall he was repairing. I thought of my father. The stones in the man's hands were as old as those my father once handled. These stones, though, had been handled before. The ones my father had worked came from his own quarry. The stones had been carted here from the temple of Artemis Gorgo at the park Christos and I had visited. I liked the idea of their reuse, of people finding another home for them, and their living on in another building. I stood in the rain, watching the mason. He wasn't young. His cement, as a result of the rain, was having a very hard time hardening.

~

I met Sophia by chance at the Gorgona, a red and white beached fishing boat near the quay. She pulled a plastic bottle of wine from her bag and offered me a swig. We walked across the quay on a concrete bridge. The sun was falling, but we didn't turn back. Instead, we headed up the island road, and when it was almost too dark to see, we turned down a set of steps we guessed would lead seaward, and gingerly felt our way down to an isolated cove.

Sophia had come to Greece to buy land together with some friends, the plan being to farm it with them. But then one of them had become ill. Both she and I were questioning, we discovered, how to support the dream of living simply.

Sophia encouraged me not to give up on my wish to find the country I remembered from my childhood sojourn—a place filled with peasants, goats, and snow-covered mountains. She assured me I could find it. Because she had been coming to Greece on and off for twenty-some years and had recently spent seven months in a small village on the Peloponnesus, I trusted her when she told me she knew how different other parts of Greece were from Corfu. She insisted that the whole country hadn't changed beyond my recollection. The next day, I bought a bus ticket.

~

At two in the morning, the giant ships in the harbor of Patras glittered, lit up like Christmas trees. Inside the bus station were just two people. One was a man sleeping, head and arms flung over one of the back tables, and the other was an attendant behind a Plexiglas window. My connecting bus to Kalamata wasn't scheduled to leave until eight-thirty. I sat down on a hard chair. The place smelled like cigarettes. I moved the ashtray in front of me to another table.

I didn't know what I was doing here and I wasn't sure where I was headed. This was so typical of the course of my life, the continual urge to leave, to seek out the next place, in hope that it might speak to me.

~

The bus wove around curves of the Greek Peloponnesus. I tried to remember the time I had bicycled these roads, but I couldn't recognize a single landmark. Erhard greeted me at the bus station. All I knew of this German olive farmer were the emails we had exchanged. How should we do this, he inquired. The Greek way?

We kissed on both cheeks.

Good ride? He asked.

I could use a restroom.

It's over there, behind the bakery. He pointed.

My body shook as I walked, each step carrying me farther from the controller who had just asked to see my ticket. I had felt sure he would ask for identification, discover my expired visa, deport me.

~

Above us were the snowcapped Taygetus Mountains. As Erhard drove, the countryside grew more and more stunning. This was the Greece I had known as a child, unpopulated save for a few small villages, houses built of stone, and the various goatherd and olive orchard. The road wound around a bend and Erhard pointed to a stone enclosure filled with sheep. That's Eftihia, the shepherdess. Her family's a strange one. Her father and two of her brothers committed suicide.

I looked down at the person standing among the sheep. She looked like me. She was dressed in Western clothes, jeans, a windbreaker, and ball cap. She waved.

She talks a lot of shit, Erhard went on. One afternoon my ex-girl-friend was lying in the bed where you're now staying and Eftihia came in and lay down beside her. I don't know if Eftihia's a lesbian or not, but you don't just do that kind of thing, walk into someone's room.

I worked that day cutting the purple, asparagus-like flower heads off an invasive rhizome. The olive orchard was craggy, rock-filled, and overlooked the sea. Wild daisies and red flowers with black eyes dotted the ground beneath the trees. I stopped snipping, the plastic crate of flow-er heads in my arms, and listened to the bells of Eftihia's sheep as they plunked and tinkled.

~

I took apart two walls of an old goat shelter on Erhard's land in two sunny half-days. The stones were heavy. I was happy lifting them—so other were they than wet bags of horse dung. I arranged the big stones in one place, flat stones in another, stones with just one face in a third. The rock was sandstone and came from a quarry visible from the road as delicate cross-cuts in the mountain's red side. You like doing that, don't you? Erhard said, taking a break from pruning to check on my progress.

Makes me feel close to my dad.

The weight in my arms registered a memory that wasn't specific, but had to do, overwhelmingly, with my stonemason father. I tossed unusable stones onto a rubble pile.

~

As I walked back to Erhard's flat one afternoon, arms aching from heavy lifting, a man on a donkey crossed the country road. I was reminded of a photograph I had recently seen of *rembetika* singer Haralambos Maltezos sitting sidesaddle on a donkey, olive switch in hand. He had been an old-time stone quarrier with shoulders as massive and hunched from years of heavy lifting as my dad's. He had run an olive mill that was turned by a horse, had lived without electricity, and had written a song about a sexy little partridge. I tried to imagine Haralambos's voice as I walked. I thought it would have to sound like the groans and hums of the sandstone quarry up the road.

~

I dug out sod from the side of the collapsed wall with a pointed shovel, moving each stone into the shade of a beautiful unpruned olive tree. The soil was red. I picked up a stone. Beneath it was a white salamander, surprised to see the sun. I loved the stone and the sun. A day ago, Erhard had confided in me his plan to install one-million-Euros-worth of solar panels on his property; the resulting power he planned to sell to the Greek electric company. I lifted another stone and carried it over to the tree. By the end of the day, I had rebuilt one side of the stone igloo where nomadic shepherds and their families had once stayed. My dry wall was rough. It bulged a bit, Erhard pointed out. You deserve some chocolate.

He held out a few squares.

~

I walked through the stone-paved town of Proastio by the village fountain complete with stone-basins for the washing of clothes and grain sacks, a number of which had been laid out to dry on the hollowed stones. Then I picked my way down a meandering walking path, thinking of Patrick Leigh Fermor's description, in *Mani: Travels in the Southern Peloponnese*, of the woman salt collector who, along with her daughter, had once scraped sea salt from the rocks here for a living. The price of salt varied from place to place and season to season, but the woman had spoken of making the equivalent of sixpence a day. There had not been a trace of bitterness in her, according to Fermor. I'm bitter, I thought, as I looked out at the sea. I was working for the rich, working for free. The salt collectors had lived in caves, gone barefoot, soaked their bread rusks in brine. I dangled my feet over the cliff. Colorful wildflowers enveloped me.

~

I recognized the beach as soon as we drove down to it. I was already out of the car, walking across the beach, studying the houses to my left, searching for any sign that one of them might be blocking a cave in the cliff. This was the beach my parents and I had come to after running over a beehive on our bikes and suffering multiple stings. I had been unable to comb my hair for the pain of the stingers still in my head. The beach was now touristed. One of the older houses was where Nikos Kazantzakis wrote *Zorba the Greek*. For a moment, I felt as if I had returned.

Late that night, I cracked open *Zorba* to the dialogue between the Buddha and the Shepherd. The back and forth spelled out my shepherdess dreams, contrasting them with my reality. I didn't have animals, land, or a husband. But one didn't, the Buddha insisted, need such things to be happy.

~

I fled Erhard's, ultimately, walking without plan, bags on my back, down a steep mountain path. After some time, I came upon a hotel near the sea. The woman who answered the bell was grey-haired and dressed in black.

She said she had a room for me and lowered her price when she saw my expression. I'm a mother, she said in Greek. I understand all children's problems.

The room was airy and clean. My hostess opened the doors and told me to sit outside on the stone balcony in the sun. She would bring me a coffee. She brushed my flushed cheek with her hand.

I looked out at the sea, grey and rolling. In minutes, she had returned with coffee, a slice of spanakopita, and two sweets. From the balcony, I watched her walk through the garden. As soon as I tasted the food she had brought, the taste of Greece, I began to cry. I cried silently, the sea mirroring me. Then the sun went down. I brought the tray inside and closed the balcony doors. I sat at a desk and avoided looking into the lit mirror. I got out my book of poems by Ritsos and finished a translation I had begun earlier that morning. Titled 'Necessary Explanations,' the poem marvels at how some poems come to an author whole, without the poet even knowing their meaning, the way a knee in the corner of a sheet can spell out some 'inexplicable quest.'

A Short History of Bubbles

A child?
I want to talk about having a baby, not having a baby, or adopting a child with you. I just wish I wasn't 58 and hadn't had a vasectomy.

Fifty-eight? How old are you, Dave? I say and laugh.

Did I just say 58?

Dave's 48. I'm 37. We're in bed. He gets up. I met Dave through a friend. He's a woodworker who manages his own high-end woodshop in Brooklyn, and the day I met him he was laying someone off. Soon he'll use my meager salary to deny me my dream of a child, but all I hear right now is water running down the hall in the bathroom. I feel incredibly sad. It isn't anything I understand. I'm thinking about my father asking me, So, I guess Dave won't want to start another family?

I'm in tears when Dave comes back to bed. His arms are wet. Water drips off his elbows onto my arms as he kisses my tears.

We drive to Van Cortlandt Park to walk Dave's dog, Seven. I feel like crying whenever I see a child. The trees are light green, having not yet leafed all the way out. In two weeks it's going to be so different here, I say, imagining the density of the leaf cover, and reaching up to touch a new, still wrinkled maple leaf.

The wrinkled leaf makes me want to cry, as does the thirteen-or-so-year-old girl who stops to ask us Seven's name.

What's on your mind? Dave asks, after we break off the path, and head into a more wooded area.

It's too hard to admit that I am reeling inside, that I suddenly want to move to the country and leave Dave and his teenage children to their lives he can't leave in the city. It's a knee-jerk reaction. I want him to have to make some concession. How can he get it all and deny me? I say, I'm thinking about the spring.

Interview

I feel fated as I walk down a cobbled street in downtown Brooklyn. The trees are large, the building old. Inside Petr's office there's a photograph of his late son, Jan, wedged within the gilded frame of a giant mirror near a desk. I went to school with Jan. I stare at his face in the photo as I sit in Petr's bottomless chair. Petr's from the Czech Republic. I want to know whether he has read Mark Slouka's *The Visible World*—the book in which the main character, a Czech woman, never recovers, despite marrying and having a child, from her hurt past. He has Milan Kundera's *Testimonies* on his shelf, loaded with post-its. I take the job, not only because I need money. I take the job, if I'm perfectly honest, because during the interview Petr confesses to me that he is no longer together with Jan's mother; he had a son out of wedlock, a boy who is now age seven. Petr is in his sixties. Dave has been telling me he is too old to have a baby.

The lid of a teapot

Work begins in the back, windowless office, under buzzing, fluorescent lights. Petr starts me on his finances, balancing budgets for a myriad of accounts. He is a meticulous record-keeper, and as he teaches me how to enter figures into the spreadsheet, whenever he comes upon an accounting error, he swears he'll kill the woman who worked the job before me. I enter numbers, decimals, and corresponding codes into the Excel documents. My eyes swim. I grow nervous, thinking I'll make some error.

Cleaning up after making a tea my second day of work, I wedge the top of Petr's teapot on so tightly I can't get it off. The lip chips as Petr pries it off. A little piece of sandpaper softens the blotched ceramic. Petr operates in a mode of perpetual panic. He sands furiously. I go back into the office and hold my breath as I add up the numbers, squinting at the miniature boxes on the screen. What mistake will I make next? What will he find to berate me about? In this year alone, I've heard from a musician, Petr has hired and fired nine personal assistants. The kindergarten next door to my office is humming with activity. Children's voices cut through the thin walls. What is lightning? I hear one child ask.

Electricity, an adult answers.

I get up. I have a question for Petr about a receipt. He's playing the flute, learning the difficult solo in Morton Feldman's *Flute and Orchestra*.

I interrupt and he shows me on the metronome how quickly he must play the five sixteenth notes in quarter time. Outside, a girl swings back and forth on a swing, keeping her own time.

Child of science (I)

The boy in the bubble was a child of science, his birth orchestrated by doctors eager to study his genetic disease, his immune system in such peril that he could not exist without medical intervention. For a time in the late '70s and early '80s, the boy was calm and cooperated within his man-made bubble. His profoundly unhinged family life spelled a kind of emotional coldness I related to as a very young person. The only child of parents who lost a child before me, I found the boy's isolation familiar, as it somehow signified not only my reality as separate from my parents' grief, but also the dead end dirt road of my childhood. The stone house my parents built by hand was a place protected from the world. Insulated within the house, my parents and I pretended we were safe.

Then one day the boy in the bubble lost it and smeared his feces all over the inside of its plastic. Not long after this, he died. He had journeyed out of the bubble on only one occasion in a special suit. Thereafter he had refused to wear the suit ever again. Leaving his bubble *and* living within it were both unbearable existences.

The tulip bulb

In the late 1500s, a Dutch botanist returned from a trip to Constantinople with a tulip bulb and stuck it in the ground. Soon after this, people in Holland began planting tulip bulbs. A bubble was, for the Dutch at this point in time, simply something to clean up with after plunging their flower-hungry hands into dirt. Then the bubonic plague struck and perhaps because the tulips' bright petals contrasted all the drear, suddenly what one had to fork over for a single tulip bulb was exactly what it cost to buy twelve farmable acres. The soaring price of bulbs led, in a matter of months, to a new crop: tulip thieves sprang up, as if overnight, and began to proliferate. Then a trade in ungrown bulbs erupted. Everything happened underground. Petals streaked like licking flames (caused by an outbreak of the tulip mosaic virus) brought in ever higher prices.

Meanwhile, the Dutch East India Company spread smallpox across Africa and Asia. In addition to taxing indigenous farmers and monopolizing slave markets, the company began to sell shares. All it took was the company's largest share-holder to be caught selling futures to shares he no longer owned and in a matter of months the company went belly up, the Dutch economy tanked, the tulips' worth bolted, and the world's first speculative bubble popped, leaving in its wake many pairs of dirty hands.

Health insurance
Wake up, migrant worker, my father calls.

I'm awake, I say. I've taken a week off from work in the city to come home to help sell berries on our small farm.

Come out here, my father says. I've got something I want to discuss with you.

I'll be out in a minute.

He's been talking to my mother about my not having health insurance. I've overheard them. They want me to research a policy. I pull on my old jeans and a T-shirt.

We all know what would have happened to this family had I been diagnosed with cancer when I wasn't insured, my father says, as soon as I join them in the kitchen. Get some.

It wouldn't be your financial responsibility if anything happened to me, I say.

Oh, sure, we'd just disown you, my mom jeers.

I leave the conversation hanging, drink my tea, and head down to the patch. It's a warm day, the sun already at burning strength. I take the damp tarp off the wooden table, fold it up, and grab some baskets. The cedar waxwings are already eating berries, a flock of about twenty of them. Their yellow bellies glint. They always pick the biggest, reddest fruit to peck at, leaving the half-eaten and scarred berries for me to dispose of.

Letter to an old flame (I)
...i am eating lychee tonight in brooklyn. the skins are darker red than i remember, tougher, and the pits—the pits i entirely forgot about. it has been a long time since i ate them for the first and only time with you. i have a

book coming out in a month. one of the essays mentions you. it is an old love song. one i hope you don't mind me singing. a way of memorializing, of making a shrine. the essay moves beyond the pain of my poems. and tonight, as i eat the lychee, i move beyond the years i've mourned. i'm writing to tell you that i am in love with a carpenter whose apartment i'm in. dave is from montana, and this last weekend he and my dad went out and cut down a dead tree. there is a whole lot of sorrow and a whole lot of happiness at once... i wanted to tell you while the news is still new. i wanted to tell you, too, that i love you, that i won't forget, that i talk to you through the forest mushrooms, through the strawberry plants as they blossom.

Stock

I ride my bike across Brooklyn in search of a branch of my Arizona bank, thinking about Dave's and my relationship. I recognize the rough spots and know all too well how thin its fabric is. By evening there's grime on my face from battling the city on my bike. It has been eight years since airplanes flew suicidally into the center of this nation's commerce, eight years since money launderers yanked their dough out of U.S. banks, particularly those Muslim investors (who repatriated one trillion dollars of investments into Middle Eastern reserves). The dollar's worth has shriveled as the price of oil continues to skyrocket alongside the price of almost everything else. The bubble I'm riding through is so gigantic it is leaving a ripple effect in its wake.

I find no bank. Everything's a foreclosure. I search and search for a branch that doesn't seem to exist. As I ride, oceans are being dredged to quicken fiber-optic cable connection speeds. These days computers trade stock with other computers at half millionths of seconds. Forget the government bailing out banks. Forget Wall Street. Trading today consists of a back and forth sending of coded instructions—algorithms—that make decisions, the same way our brains might tell us who to love. Computers, so programmed, obviously lack judgment—they simply traffic information, battling each other to outtrade and outfake. If enough algorithms ever go rogue at the same time (and they do go rogue—sometimes making million-dollar mistakes), financial institutions will collapse in microseconds.

I would like to raise a child

I want to raise a child in the forest amidst tent worms, mud heaves, trillium, Indian paintbrush. I cannot imagine another way. Dave tells me that maybe he wants and needs to stay in the city. We are walking across Prospect Park at night. I feel something inside me clam up. My instinct is to run.

Then, on the way home, I come up with a compromise. Buy a building in the city and have my baby, I tell Dave.

He doesn't say anything.

Ben

Petr picks up his seven-year-old son Ben from the airport. Ben has traveled alone to New York from the Czech Republic. He's been awake 48 hours, Petr marvels.

He feeds the video of Ben's recent school theatrical performance into the main computer's disk drive. That's the wife seducing Joseph, Petr says, pointing to the screen and laughing. Look at the costumes.

The costumes are stunning. I rave with Petr, because this is how one gets along with Petr—one agrees.

I am no longer the calm, composed, longhaired girl who arrived at Petr's office early this spring. He's gotten under my skin. I've hacked my hair off. Now I'm used to his giving me orders, barking out commands, playing dictator. The building smells of freshly polished floors. Ben says something in Czech. Petr laughs and translates what Ben said: The technicolor coat stank.

I feel my headache ease. We watch the show and eat watermelon. Ben spills his soda and grows fearful. I whisper that he shouldn't worry; Petr hasn't seen.

At noon the next day Petr decides that we should work at his house. The three of us set off on our respective bikes. Ben needs air in his tire, so we stop at a gas station on Atlantic Avenue. The attendants say they don't have any air for bikes, but Petr insists. They reluctantly chance the use of their car tire pump after Petr agrees not to sue should Ben's tire pop. The tire fills up perfectly. Ben is eager to ride. We coast down the street. Leaving the station, I see Ben dragging his foot along the pavement to slow himself down. I fear he'll twist an ankle, break a foot. When Petr stops at the bank, I teach Ben how to brake.

A man on the train

A kind-looking man and I get on the wrong subway train and sit there until a cleaning woman tells us that we want the train on the opposing platform. We shuffle to the other train, seat ourselves, and wait. I ask what work the man does. He says construction. It's a hard time, he tells me. He is a union worker and nobody is hiring union anymore. From forty men, his company has been downsized to five.

You must be good, then, I say, as the train begins to move.

But I have to work overtime to make enough to pay my babysitter, he says, and there's no overtime, so I went to my boss and I told him, I said, I have two girls at home. I might have to leave. I have to work overtime. And he said, We'll work something out. I'm lucky, the man says, looking at me. I really am.

Does your wife work?

She left me. One day I came home and she wasn't there. You don't know how horrible that was. She got caught up with the wrong crowd. Drugs.

Oh, I'm sorry, I tell him.

I don't wish anyone to go through that kind of pain. And now my kid's school closed. She was going to a Catholic school and no one can afford tuition anymore. And then yesterday I found a new babysitter, too. The last one wasn't good. This one's from my country. And my oldest, she said, She's a good person, Daddy. I can talk with her.

Where are you from?

Ecuador.

Ecuador, I echo.

My stop is coming up. I stand up and touch his shoulder. The doors to the car open and I feel myself hesitate.

Debt-slaves

On the other side of the world, small farmers are having an increasingly hard time competing with agribusinesses on the global market. Many are now in debt and so deeply troubled they drink pesticides or drown themselves. Suicide isn't the only response to debt-slavery. After the World Bank's restructuring of the agricultural system in the 1990s, the international coffee market crashed, and Rwanda, a country whose main export was coffee, went bankrupt, its public services collapsed, and its national debt nearly doubled. The World Bank offered loans and these loans were used not to repair the damaged coffee trade but by both the Tutsi Rwandan Patriotic Army and the Hutu *Interhamwe* to purchase weapons. Everyone knows what happened next.

As it is now, farmers who aren't killing themselves, or other people, are being killed by U.S. drones. Fred Moten and Stefano Harney trace the creation of the drone to modern logistics which was itself founded upon commodities called slaves whose production was in circulation and distribution as property that reproduced and realized itself.

I fall in love
It's the way Ben jumps on me, burr-like. It's his need for physical affection. It's his hair—the curls at the base of his neck; the way Petr applies sunscreen, slathering the cream everywhere, Ben patiently extending an arm. Your hand, Petr demands.

Now can we go to the park?

At the park, Ben throws an acorn at a squirrel, and—incredibly it seems to Ben and me—the squirrel darts over, picks the acorn up in its mouth, and scampers up the tree trunk with it. Over near the swings, a man waves a four-foot-long bubble wand. Bubbles, bubbles, get your bubbles, he shouts.

Kids dance. Ben runs over, popping every one before anyone else can. A girl cries. Get your bubbles, the man shouts again.

That, I tell Dave when I get home, is the perfect job: bubble man.

Viral infections
A research fellow at Reading University implants a virus-infected chip into his hand. To prove a point, he has lab computers scan his hand. In so doing, the virus in the man's hand implants itself into the database and begins to replicate. The bionic man makes known that those with viral-infected implants risk infecting other devices. Fetal monitors have already been infected by malware. Boston's Beth Israel Hospital is battling for a cyber-secure facility. To fight the evils of the Internet, the hospital's chief information officer says, not only do you have to have a moat, you have to have a drawbridge, burning oil to pour on attackers, and guys with arrows.

I crash

Two guys pick me and my bike up. One has alcohol wipes, toilet paper. I black out. When I come to, my eyesight is strangely tunneled. Everything has become too difficult. I don't want to work anymore for Petr. I am tired of being yelled at and being told things are my mistakes.

I cry near the East River

Say, you all right? a guy walking his dog asks me.

Yeah, I'm fine, I say, raising my head from my arms.

I've been crying, trying to give up things I've never had. I am sitting in the spot where a sea of onions slept outside unprotected for several nights a few weeks back. Now a load of garlic rots one block over in a dumpster. 'We starve amidst giant granaries,' a poet once wrote.

Ben pops bubbles

Ben pops shipping bubbles. Petr talks of death, how one doesn't decide one's time, forgets one's wife's birthday, grows old, watches everyone die. Natural, he says and smiles. That's why all the Slovakian women wear black. They are all the time mourning.

Ben believes in the power of transformers, leaps up stairs, locks himself in the playground, and cries. I cry at the cream he tries to whip from milk in a cup in the office's pseudo-kitchen near the old piano. How we can love and be tricked; how we can trick ourselves; how the trick is sometimes what's real.

Petr hits the chair in anger and uses scissors to scratch his back. I dream of lost receipts, getting in trouble. I am much more than this, I want to yell. I do yell. I throw pens at Petr. He turns benevolent. I have stood up to the lion.

I compose my own replacement ad

By the time I write my own replacement ad, I have done what Petr's asked me to do: I have fiddled with his finances, defrosted his refrigerator, traveled to the Czech Republic with him for a month. I have taped parts of scores together, searched for lost trombones. I've listened, visibly sickened, as he spouts theories about how blacks are slow because they come from warmer climates. I now have nightmares of placing musicians' sheet music on the wrong stands. Each time I wake, Dave comforts me. We find each other again, after not recognizing one another's voices on the phone, after a month apart, after acknowledging that our futures are incompatible.

I am on my way to Petr's to attend to the last of it when my front bike tire sinks into a grate. I sail over my handlebars, land on my face, leave a puddle of blood on the sidewalk, and walk home knowing I've shattered my two front teeth.

Foam

Like a horse inhaling as another horse kicks her, the world, as I see it, is suffering from a condition not unlike subcutaneous emphysema, a sickness during which air bubbles proliferate beneath the skin. ('The structural implication of the current earth-encompassing network—with all its eversions into the virtual realm—is...not so much a globalization as a foaming,' writes Peter Sloterdijk. 'In foam worlds,' he adds, 'individual bubbles are not absorbed into a single, integrative hyper-orb, as the metaphysical conception of the world, but rather drawn together to form irregular hills.') But whereas every other country has to borrow against the money within its own bubbling borders, the U.S. (the horse that kicks) maintains the reserve currency of the world, because it has a privilege no other country has; it can borrow against the total amount of dollars in global circulation.

A man with needles sentences me

I borrow against what I know to be true and follow Dave's direction. He sentences me to acupuncture. I don't want to go. I stall my entrance to the subway. Underground, a boy mirrors my fear. He wears thick glasses. It is his first time riding the train. He looks scared. I tell him he is brave.

It's wobbly, he says.

The appointment isn't hard. But my second visit, a week later, hurts like hell. I leave and tears fall. The needles have evidenced my hope against hope, calling it out as fraudulent. I won't have a baby with Dave; he isn't making it happen. I fall apart. I search wildly for adoption information, but am stopped at every site by my age, Dave's marital status (he's separated, still married), and my lack of real income and absolutely no savings. Each site drives Dave farther away.

Dave, Oscar, and I deliver a table
Dave has to deliver a $45,000 table his workers have made. I do not want to be alone. I am in denial that our relationship is over, and I beg to come along for the ride. Dave rents the biggest U-Haul he can find and picks me up on Kent Avenue near the Sunbelt construction mural. I climb up into the cab. Oscar, one of Dave's employees, moves over into the middle of the front seat, so that he's sitting nearest Dave, to make room for me. Sitting between us, Oscar talks about the snow outside, his first. He tells us that his daughter, a freshman at Florida State, recently came to visit. She had never seen snow before either. She had a blast making snow angels in the middle of Fifth Avenue. But look at it now? It's dirty, Oscar says. I would stay here if they would find a way to get rid of the snow.

As we drive upstate, Oscar rambles on about how blue the snow is in the country and about how much he loves his daughter, how he paid for her college ten years in advance; paid it all, even the cost of her dorm room and books. I look over at Dave, but he's concentrated on the road. In the living room of the client's mansion, I hand Oscar the screws. He lies on his back in his T-shirt and jeans on the expensive, dark-blue carpet and screws the absurdly ornate table together.

After the table is in place, after we've broken a Tiffany's Christmas tree ornament, after the doors to the mansion close, we ride back to the city, unload the blankets from the truck, and go out for a drink. It is then in the flickering candlelight that Oscar tells us the real reason he doesn't want to stay in New York. It isn't the snow or the cold. He is lonely. He left his wife because she didn't want any more children. He always wanted more than one. He doesn't know now, though, whether he made the right decision. Dave touches my leg under the table. I am crying, but it's dark in the bar. I don't think anyone can see. Oscar seems to shrink on his stool in his beige-colored jacket and his stocking cap. He carries himself as if apologetically: this man who wants more and has lost everything, save for his daughter. He's going back to Florida to be near her.

Snowboarding
I don't want to join the ranks of Dave's wife and his girlfriend-before-me both of whom tried to snowboard just to please him, but I end up going, because Lucy, Dave's 15-year-old daughter, asks me to. What if you don't

have a choice? is how she asks. And because she never really asks me to do anything (in fact, she once asked me not to go to her soccer games), I go.

I get on the board. I spend two days proving that I can do this thing. On the second day, after I go down the bunny hill without falling, I take the board off and sit outside near the garbage can on the people-filled deck in the sun. I wonder, as I sit, feet cramped in my rented boots, whether I've lost myself. What am I doing? Sure, I've learned something—learned to carve the snow with my body, learned to twist in anticipation of the slope. I've even stopped fearing being ankle-cuffed. But something is wrong. What is it about these days—days I've told Dave and Lucy to go enjoy themselves on their boards, days I've fought my inner battles outwardly with the mountain—that hurts?

The lift man watches. He says, It's beautiful watching you out there.

He sees me learn while Dave is elsewhere, on some difficult trail.

Lucy and I drink bubble tea
Lucy's loaded her straw with tapioca balls. A man with a piece of pizza in his mouth walks past. She spits and the balls just miss him. I run across the street and slip behind the outer plastic wall of the bodega where the flowers are. Lucy chases me, a newly loaded straw full of bubbles in her mouth.

Letter to an old flame (II)
...the sides close in, the city and its expenses, no insurance, always the homeless, the concrete that covers and encloses. i try to find its other side... sometimes i think that the road was never going to be easy, that i would always have to walk the mile in, through snow up to my thighs, that there wouldn't be light when i got there, it would be cold... a man who lives behind a fence in a car shovels snow from behind the dumpster. sometimes i see him doing pushups on the sidewalk, bare-handed in this weather. now the reality is my only having my duffle. how many times must i leave. how many times must i begin again... i want to be okay. i want the fact that maybe i can never be a mother to be okay. i want the city to be okay. i spoke to an old friend today. she said, people die. you don't want to not talk to them. so i am writing...

We watch Trombone Shorty
We watch Trombone Shorty on the Internet. Dave says, Look, I think he's doing circular breathing. His cheeks are puffed, his breathing made visible only in the thrust of his shoulders. His eyes bulge. Lucy, who is usually so composed, goes and gets a glass, fills it with water, and hunts down what she calls Spring's straw—my bubble tea straw. As Trombone Shorty continues to play, Lucy, a trombonist herself, blows bubbles continuously, breathing through her nose, collecting the air in her cheeks, trying to pace her exhales so the bubbles surface evenly.

Child of science (II)
Julian Assange—today's child of science—compares system administrators to yesteryear's industrial workers who once made up the backbone of the world's economy. 'The interconnected power of system administrators is,' Assange lectures, 'an order of magnitude different. Today, a single system administrator alone has unimaginable power.' An administrator like Assange draws air out of the foam of the state, breathing it back into the commons. And what does it mean to infiltrate national systems, to spell out relations between body and state? It means this child of science is hunted and trapped—as if within a bubble—inside another nation's embassy.

Back into the commons
It's snowing again. I walk Dave's dog down Kent Avenue. Dave's in Utah, snowboarding with Lucy. The snow whisks around the cranes on the construction mural. I recall the feeling of being glued to the board, of letting the earth turn me—before I learned to turn myself this way and that, as if throwing a clay pot with my body. How many others, I wonder, are out there, similarly not knowing what they are doing, flinging themselves here and there, wishing for someone to love them? For better or worse, maybe this is all there is, I think, no answer, no question, just algorithmic motion and drone reproduction. I step around a urine-dotted snowdrift. Suddenly Seven leaps up, takes the leash in his mouth and begins shaking his head, jerking me back and forth. He is telling me, I know, to let go. But I keep walking with him. We are almost home.

An Era of the Terror of Terror

> In this age of terror and the terror *of* terror...
> —Patricia Hampl

In one of the last photographs Chris Hondros shot before being fatally wounded in a mortar attack in Misurata, two Libyan rebels pose with guns. One of them wears Nike sweatpants. The swoosh is easy to see. Hondros painted with light in cramped quarters. So close was he to these men who were storming a loyalist stronghold, he had to fish-eye the scene. Given the lack of space, the utter non-depth of field, there finally is no separation, artistically, between him and the rebels.

Flashback to the dead of the night at an Iraqi checkpoint outside Mosul. Samar Hassan screams, her dress splattered with her parents' blood. Here, Hondros stands back. The child is alone in terror. Samar had been riding in the car with her family as they hurried home after visiting relatives, trying to make the checkpoint before curfew. Then U.S. Apache Company soldiers opened fire.

When I first saw this photograph, I didn't register the flower print of Samar's dress. I didn't yet know of her brother Rakan, shot in the spine at the checkpoint that night, who would lose the ability to walk.

The Apache Company soldiers were, as is so often the case, cleared of any wrongdoing.

If it were up to me, I'd kill the Americans and drink their blood, Samar's older sister Jilan commented, when a reporter later found her, Samar, Rakan, and their younger brother living at their uncle's.

This was before Rakan was flown to the United States for an operation to help him walk again and before he was killed when a mortar struck their uncle's house.

What a mess there is in Afghanistan, Iraq, Syria, and Libya now, and what a mess was made of Samar's life. I see her looking at Hondros's photo of her on the night of her parents' murder. Another reporter has again tracked her down and is showing her this image she has never seen—her terrified scream captured by a photographer who is now another casualty in a string of endless casualties.

A Short History of Reading
Anti-War Literature with Cadets

Black Hearts

My first day teaching at a private military college, I wore a short skirt and a wide-brimmed hat. I didn't yet know that neither was permitted attire. Entering my classroom, a student asked, Are you new here, too?

I am your professor.

The kid's face reddened, and then he turned and disappeared quickly into a sea of uniforms. As I handed out syllabi, I surveyed the room. There was only one female student, and she was also one of the only students of color. There was similarly only one civilian, a kid dressed in sweats. The rest were rooks—incoming freshmen who intended to become cadets. In this class, I was assigning *Black Hearts*—Jim Frederick's journalistic account of the rape and murder of Abeer al-Janabi, a 14-year-old Iraqi girl, and the murder of her family.

We would start the semester, I told the students as soon as they were seated at their desks, by writing about a conflict in our own lives. Then we would gradually expand that paper to include research. Throughout the semester we would be talking about war—one of the greater conflicts. At some point, we would interrupt our reading of *Black Hearts* to skim Euripides's play, *The Trojan Women*, an ancient story of war and rape. The legal acknowledgement of rape as a strategic act of torture had been ruled by an international court for the first time in world history not even two decades ago. Hundreds of thousands of women had been raped—many by soldiers who knew they were HIV positive—during the genocide in Rwanda. I explained to the class how this, and those rapes perpetrated during the genocide in Bosnia, had changed court rulings. In any case, what is the consequence today for a soldier who participates in such an ancient wartime ritual? I queried.

The class was silent. Well, I told them, read about Private Steven D. Green, the 24-year-old soldier who raped and murdered Abeer al-Janabi; he was sentenced to life in prison.

Before me sat 23 young people, all but one dressed in the same blue uniform with their covers on their desks, their spit-shined shoes black and luminescent. Their hair was shorn to match the protocol of their respective platoons, save for the one girl who wore her hair, according to regulations, in a bun just above the nape of her neck. Outside, the sun shone. For many, this was their first ever college class. Their names and faces mixed as they talked.

It would be weeks before I knew their names and stories. Weeks before I would recognize John at the far end of the classroom, a driven wrestler, who took copious notes and refused to receive help for his learning disability so as not to be dismissed from the military and lose his scholarship. Behind John was Lewis, a football player from Florida who came from a feuding family. Directly in front of me sat Fergus who had come clean with the help of God; behind him sat Addison with his quick wit; at Addison's left was Ralph with his thick-framed glasses and finely tuned moral compass; Lobo sat behind him, and Don, to the far left, quiet, eyebrows knitted. At the back of the room by the windows, Dustin wooed Liz. She was Mexican-American, petite and beautiful, even in her boxy uniform.

~

I have a .22. Shooting it is the next best thing to sex.

I stood among a group of young female faculty in a ballroom at a required faculty event, drinking wine. I like a revolver, another woman responded. You can't miss.

I shot a M16 one time, someone else bragged.

I should have a party; we can shoot off my porch, the woman with the .22 said.

Stay with us; don't run away now, a colleague begged, holding onto my arm.

I hung around the ballroom a little while longer and then excused myself.

~

Black Hearts is good. I've read ahead, Fergus greeted me.

Yeah, it's really good, Addison said, nodding.

I was flabbergasted. I had expected students to protest its contents. They were telling me, though, that they loved the book. I've never read anything in school that applies to my life before, John said.

Yeah, and this is the first real depiction of war I've ever read, Addison added.

I feel like I'm really there, Don echoed.

I had assumed that these kids would be hooked on real war stories; that they would be experts at what it meant to choose the lives they were signing up for. I had two simultaneous thoughts: their naiveté gave me leeway and I had a job to do; I had to educate them.

Later, as we brainstormed potential personal conflicts to write about, John suggested that he write about the Afghan police, who, he thought, were not doing their job of helping the U.S. implement democracy in Afghanistan.

I had to bite my tongue. I was interested in John's view. I encouraged him. You're thinking on a global scale—that's great, I said. But feel free to write about something more personal—even though I know that conflict is personal to you. You know what I mean, don't you?

Breyten raised his hand. He was rattled by his brother's deployment, he said. It was bringing up the emotions he had experienced when his family had been separated during their move to the U.S. What about separation from families? I asked. Can you guys identify with that conflict?

Students nodded. Many of them came from military families and had been separated from their fathers for months, even years at a time. Then Lewis spoke up. This is my first time away from home, he said. It's hard. We only get to talk to our families for ten minutes a week.

Really? I asked.

As rooks, we don't have privileges, Addison explained.

I knew the freshmen in uniform were being tested, but I had no idea to what extent. They had to square the corners everywhere they walked, woke at five, and PT'ed three times a week, even when the weather was bad. One student had told me that they weren't allowed to decorate their rooms, had to chew their food a certain number of times per meal, and only after two semesters, could they win the privilege to use their cell phones.

I asked everyone to take out a sheet of paper and begin drafting a proposal for their first paper. Lewis raised his cast. He had injured his wrist playing football. I'll help you write, I said, and went to him.

For the next ten minutes, he dictated a story to me about how his grandpa was suing his father. There was a possibility of his not being able to afford college. He spoke in a whisper.

Some students volunteered to share their conflicts at the end of the period. Dillon spoke about his father's alcoholism; Earl talked about being worried he wouldn't know how to balance family and business when he took over his father's machine shop, and Eliot wanted to know whether he could write about love. Of course, I said.

What's your conflict, Professor? Addison wanted to know.

I'm 38 and I want to have kids. My boyfriend has two, and doesn't want more, I said.

You can adopt, someone suggested.

We had gone over our fifty-minute class time. There was a flurry of chair scraping. Two kids stayed after class to talk to me about border issues. One student had grown up on a ranch in Arizona and experienced the negative effects of illegal aliens, as he called them, on his small town's economy. He was tall and blond-haired and blushed as he spoke.

Liz stood behind him, waiting. If she heard him, her face didn't belie her emotions. After he left, she asked whether she could write about gang violence on the border. I didn't know it then, but she would write about how in high school she had been kidnapped by gang members at gunpoint.

~

They're really bad off, the guys in here that enlisted, John was saying.

John was right. Protagonist Steven Green came from a broken family.

It was hard, students complained, to keep all the platoon members and officers and commanders in *Black Hearts* straight.

I agreed—there were too many names in the book. But when I asked about Sergeant Tony Yribe, students knew who he was. He was a muscle man. They wanted to be like him, cool, calm, and collected, not like

Green, a poor, drooling rapist, who had come unraveled after several of his platoon buddies had been killed. I wondered what they would come to think of Yribe by the time they finished reading the book.

~

'Okay, I am going to give you a summary of what happened to me while I was over in Dodge, asking Liz on a Rookie Date,' Dustin's email began. He and I now corresponded regularly, but this, I noted, wasn't just an email to me; he'd copied it to everyone in his platoon.

> I was expecting to sing a song and then maybe do some PT, but no, the entire platoon got to ask me one question each. So, the first few questions were pretty benign, but then I got asked 'how big my balls were'... And another recruit told me that I could take Liz on a 'rookie date,' if he got to take my sister on a date. Another recruit started screaming in my face and asking me to recite the enlisted ranks of the Marine Corps (JROTC Hitler). Along the other wall, I was asked if I would win in a fight against Rct. Leno, so I answered truthfully and said probably not. Farther down, I was ridiculed for 'smelling bad,' even though I had applied deodorant, shaved and applied aftershave. Finally, towards the end, one recruit asked me if I was a 'good Christian boy and had read the Bible.' Seeing as I am not Christian, I answered that I was not a good Christian boy, that I was an atheist (which was a lie, because I didn't feel like explaining my Wiccan religion to a bunch of hostile Neanderthals), so they ridiculed me further because I was an atheist that doesn't like to fight. One of the SSgts asked me if 'my mom knew that I was gay.' Not only was that a complete lack of respect in every form (which by the way, he was dancing around me the whole time, pretending to kick me in the balls, to see if I would react), but it was also just socially offensive... Basically, the moral of the story is, if another recruit from another platoon comes and asks to take one of our rook sisters on a 'rookie date,' or to regi ball, please don't be stupid... It makes you all look like retarded cave men/women, and makes that recruit not want to deal with the stupidity. All in all, I'm not sure I want to go back and ask for her to go to regimental ball,

because the whole endeavor was basically a big dick measuring
contest, and I am by no means a cocky cave man.
I shut my computer down. I knew Dustin had been spending time with Liz,
but I hadn't known what it meant to try to date a rook from another platoon. There was so much needless sexual shaming in the world. I wanted
to protect him, but I didn't know how.

~

Their hair was collectively shorter. Everyone got a buzz cut this weekend,
Ralph informed me of the obvious as I walked into the classroom.

'Brazen head' was written on the blackboard, left there, I assumed,
from the class before ours. The sun was shining as I handed out a *Black
Hearts* quiz.

I've forgotten what sleep is, Willie complained.

I had gone overboard preparing the quiz. There were eighteen
questions. Answer as many as you can, I said. Don't freak out if you don't
get through them all.

Students labored over the quiz. Fergus stayed on, after the class
had ended, answering the last of the questions.

Reading the quizzes, the general consensus seemed to be that
Black Hearts served as a guidebook for how *not* to lead troops. 'I found it
to be a tragic, yet empowering account of the dedication these men had
to their post, even when they had no support but each other,' one student
wrote. Higher ups, most students agreed, hadn't cared enough about those
they were leading into battle. Another student explained, 'I have realized
that leaders may be a higher rank, but they still need to respect and listen
to those that are subordinate to themselves. They also need to lead on and
off the battlefield...with confidence.' Overall, everyone thought that Green's
crime could have been avoided, if only Green—not to mention his company—had received some kind of help.

~

Twelve U.S. soldiers were facing charges relating to the killing of three innocent Afghani civilians. I heard the news on my drive home from the college.

The soldiers had, in two cases, thrown grenades at the innocent victims (to create the illusion that they were under attack), and then shot them. After the first murder happened, one specialist had messaged his father on Facebook to say that he was scared that it was just a matter of time before he was pressured to partake in subsequent murders. I crested the hilltop overlooking the town where I lived, listening closely as the specialist's father told reporters about how, after chatting online with his son, he had called an inspector general, a senator, a sergeant, the Army's criminal investigation division, and even a command center, but hadn't received one helpful reply. His son was now one of the men facing criminal charges in collusion with these murders. I shivered as I drove. The resonances between these killings and those murders recounted in *Black Hearts* were frightening.

~

If the college fires me, it might be the best thing that could happen, I thought, as I shook Eliot's parents' hands. I had just shut *Redacted* off halfway through the film. Dustin had suggested we watch it in class. Because it was based on the rape and murder we were reading about in *Black Hearts*, I had ordered it. It was parents' day, but I hadn't known. Eliot's parents had settled in the back of the room at the beginning of class, their presence making me more and more nervous as the language in the film grew progressively more heinous, until finally I had gotten up and said, I don't think I can show any more of this.

Eliot came from a religious background—he was writing his conflict paper about the difference between romance and marriage. What did you say your name was again, Eliot's father asked me on the way out of the room.

I was dancing with fire and I knew it. But I had always assigned controversial texts, always provoked students to wrestle difficult subject matter. Still, I knew enough to say that I wasn't going to show the second-half of the film in class, even though students wanted to see it. I would show it, I informed them, when I could make it optional to attend.

~

The argument made in *Black Hearts* is that the rape and murder of Abeer al-Janabi, and the murder of her family was the result of a platoon's difficult deployment, I lectured. Ultimately, the author questions why some people break under pressure, whereas others maintain their composure. His argument is that the ringleader of this crime, Private Steven Green was racist, unloved, and bullied; he had a criminal record and had been let into the Army on a moral waiver. Basically, he is saying that Green was mentally unstable and couldn't handle the violence he witnessed in Iraq. What do you guys think?

I wasn't convinced that the crime hinged on Green's personality disorder; in my eyes, the war itself was on trial. I stood behind the wooden podium. Through the windows in front of me, I could see students making tight, right-angled turns wherever the sidewalk forked. Already, even though class had just started, students were falling asleep at their desks. Never before, in my seven years teaching at the college level, had students fallen asleep on me, but they did here, en masse, each class. I like your shoes, Fergus said, straying off topic by commenting on my yellow clogs.

I heard shiny is in, I said, throwing him a grin.

It is, he said, thrusting his spit-shined shoe out from under his chair.

I changed my tactic; I had to get discussion going. What do you all think of Yribe now? I asked. On their midterms, students had overwhelmingly backed Sergeant Tony Yribe for his cool, even after he accidentally shot and killed someone at a checkpoint. Today, though, I was interested in whether they had changed their minds. They had read enough now to learn that Yribe doesn't rat on Green, even after Green confesses to al-Janabi's rape and murder. If you were Yribe, would you snitch on Green, or not? I asked.

Ralph, a student who had taken a life-changing trip to a mosque with his Episcopalian high school church group and who generally questioned things, was first to answer: I would rat.

We'd snitch, other students agreed.

Saying this took courage; they were all feeling the pressure of adhering to the honor code that required they report on those who broke school rules, a code that often was in direct conflict with the loyalty they'd sworn to their rook brothers and sisters. How will you know whether it's the right thing to do or not? I asked.

I pushed students to envision how they each might handle the stress of combat. How, I wanted to know, had they come to believe in war? How did they rationalize it? Invited to articulate their own morals, students' answers came out as clichés. Honor, someone said.

Integrity.

I want to serve my country, protect my family.

Enact the will of God.

This was pure, unadulterated, religious and patriotic speak. What, I wanted to ask them, was integrity? What might it mean to really live toward something like duty?

'Your body speaks its mind,' Dietrich Bonhoeffer, who was hanged for attempting to kill Hitler, said. 'We have been silent witnesses of evil deeds...intolerable conflicts have worn us down and even made us cynical...[W]ill our...honesty with ourselves [be] remorseless enough...?' I had tacked this quote above my desk.

~

Papers flowed in. The conflicts my students were writing about ranged from effects of sleep deprivation (in one military study, giraffes were the subject of research, as they only slept 1.9 hours a night) to the environmental effects of off-roading. One of my favorite essays was Breyten's. It was a letter to his brother in Afghanistan. In the letter, Breyten tells his brother that he is thinking non-stop about him, wondering if he will come back, and what it will be like when he does return, if he'll be different, or whether war will have stolen his best friend. Liz's paper was about shooting herself with her brother's black 9mm gun. I didn't know whether, in actuality, this had happened, as Liz confessed that she had changed certain details in this paper to protect herself, but what I took from her essay was that she, like so many others at this university, was a young person whose life had been surrounded and altered by violence. Again and again I wondered, as I read students' writings, whether I could place myself between their already destabilized positions and the military's greed, and whether I could transform their potential to war into an ability to hold their individual selves accountable.

~

It was the time of freshman plague. Everyone was worn down and sick. Meanwhile, enrollment in the military was soaring with the depressed economy, despite the fact that this year again more soldiers had killed themselves than had been killed in Iraq. Winter bit my cheeks. I tied my hair back. The day before Thanksgiving, one cadet raised his hand. What are we doing over there in Iraq and Afghanistan? Why are we killing children? Why are we getting killed? You've got to wonder, he said.

The class on its own was discussing war. Students had been moved by the images of children killed during the Iraq war that flashed on screen at the end of *Redacted*. I had finally showed the film, after putting it off. Several students hadn't attended the voluntary viewing—Eliot among them. But many had. The film was a simplistic portrayal of a complex event, I'd commented, and students had agreed. But maybe that was the point. War was deadly and some soldiers lacked morality. I'd already seen most of the images Brian De Palma sampled at the end of the film, but my students hadn't. I sat there, listening to them talk. Ralph was really questioning. Dustin was, I could tell, listening hard. He sat forward in his seat and raised his hand. There will always be war, because it's needed for peace, just like there is light and dark.

Elie countered him, I don't think we have to have war.

What are we doing over there? Ralph asked again. Why do we go kill people?

~

Wikileaks leaked a new cache of 250,000 secret intelligence documents from embassies around the world, and almost simultaneously the site's founder Julian Assange was accused of rape. One congressman called for WikiLeaks to be reclassified as a terrorist organization. The leak, he claimed, was worse than a military attack.

Emails arrived like hotcakes in my inbox calling for public outcry. 'Ever wonder why the media so rarely gives the full story of what happens behind the scenes?' one email read. 'This is why—because when they do, governments can be vicious in their response.' Meanwhile, the college issued prohibitions against accessing Wikileaks on campus computers, and military personnel were cautioned against accessing the website on their personal computers. Executive Order 13526 reasoned that this caution was related to the requirement for cadets and midshipmen to pass a security clearance before they commissioned, and that 'an individual's commission could...be in jeopardy, depending on the content of the accessed material.' Students could, however, the order continued, 'speak freely about Wikileaks within the confines of a closed classroom, but they were prohibited from speaking in a public forum on these topics.'

Reading the order, I thought of my students' limited exposure to information that wasn't censored or filtered. What really was the risk of anyone being informed that the State Department had instructed diplomats to spy on other diplomats, or that the Saudi royal family was urging the U.S. to attack Iran? Shouldn't members of a democracy have a right to know these things? Shouldn't kids being trained to kill for their country watch those who had gone through such training gun down persons on the ground from the relative safety of a military helicopter?

I took out the exams on *Black Hearts* that I had just administered and began scanning them. 'The only individuals who truly failed were Green and his three counterparts. Yet the fact remains that no one else resorted to such an extreme outlet [as rape and murder], even though they were under the same [stressful] conditions. The real problem was that the soldiers lost faith in the system they were fighting for, because that system unduly lost faith in them. To say that discipline is what binds them together would be a lie; they simply had nothing to fight for,' Jessie had scrawled.

'What did it mean to lose faith in a system, a country, your higher ups, your brothers? Once they cease to be moral in nature, the men themselves need to be pulled from action,' Tom had written in his spiky handwriting, adding, 'There is a point where restoring discipline is not the issue and providing a level-headed fighting force is... The last thing you want is a psychologically unstable soldier running around with a loaded gun... There really is not a set or specified way to lead these kinds of soldiers that have had previous criminal records. Experience and experimenting with different styles in this situation is really the only way.' Jay suggested that 'Green could have been...sat down...and then [given] a good motivational talk... The only thing [soldiers] need instilled in them is that they have someone there for them. To look out for their safety, to bring them home, to care for their lives more than the mission, and finally, that they have someone to confide in.'

Within four years, some of my students would, I knew, find themselves in just such situations—leading others, even younger and more innocent, into combat. I was beginning to learn what it meant to have military in one's blood. I was beginning to learn what it took to numb oneself. The change in some of my freshmen was undeniable; in just a few months' time they had checked out.

Why are you here? Breyten asked me on the last day of class. Why did you come here to teach?

I know why, Addison answered for me. They hired you because you're nurturing and they know we need that.

Mother Courage and Her Children
Is war about profit? I asked the class.

I was sitting on my desk. Dustin was seated to my right, and Liz, no longer sitting next to him, was in the far right row near the window. Many of my former students had signed up for my class again. I was happy to see their faces mixed in among other unfamiliar ones. Outside, the snow piled up ever higher, drifts in places taller than I was.

Yes, the class answered almost in unison.

What do you make of Brecht's statement that war teaches people nothing?

It's not true, Jeremiah said. Jeremiah was a new student for me. He sat in the second row from the whitewashed block wall, behind Jordan. His face was round and his gaze penetrating. I grew up in Pennsylvania, in Amish country, and my boss back home is a Quaker, Jeremiah continued. He and I have discussions all the time about war. I mean, can we live without war, especially when the ideologies like those of Nazi Germany or Imperial Japan can't be reasoned with? Both of these societies were built on irrational and racist ideas.

A civilian student interrupted. The way Brecht looks at war as this evil, deceitful, and avoidable thing that we dress up as a glamorous necessity is interesting, she said. Why did you decide to teach this book?

I talked about rhetoric, drew the triangle on the board, circling the reader's role, and spoke about the first time I had read the play. Brecht attempts to alienate his readers to make them think, rather than to allow them to identify romantically with his characters, I added.

~

Jeremiah was looking down at his desk. I had just read his essay on *Mother Courage* and it had stunned me; in it, he admitted that a moment in class had him questioning war:

The play *Mother Courage and Her Children* was written by Bertolt Brecht before the outbreak of the Second World War. He wrote it on the run for his life from Nazi Germany. The major theme in the play is that war is wrong. For the past month in class war has been debated and my opinion on war was very steadfast. I believed that war was necessary and...right. There have only been a few people in the class that did not believe this. Most of them have spoken their opinion, but have been cowardly about it. These few people know they are at a military college and they are outnumbered. They must think that their opinions will not matter to most of their fellow students and will not make an impact, but it has.

There was this 'are you serious' look that I saw from you (Professor Ulmer). Forgive me for the assumption I am going to make, because the rest of my paper is going to be on this. For the past month or so you have played devil's advocate for the anti-war position, for which there has not been much support. You have been very professional and have not shown any emotion, except once. The discussion was about how the purpose of war is not to kill people, but to just stop them. I had made a comment and another student had done the same. Then for a split second when the attention of the class was on a student in the back of the room I saw an expression on your face. It was a 'are you serious' expression. I interpreted this as: can he really believe what he just said? This expression stuck with me, and when writing my paper I could not forget it. I thought the situation over and over again in my head. I thought about what I said, and how emotionless it was. How I had sounded like an asshole. It made me think, how can I be a Christian, but so detached from another human?

I remembered the day Jeremiah was invoking. He had made the comment that war wasn't about killing people, just stopping them, and I had interjected and given an example out of *Restrepo*—a film students had recommended that I watch. What about that scene in *Restrepo* where one of the soldiers in Afghanistan is celebrating his first kill? I had asked.

Throughout the rest of his essay Jeremiah had questioned his plan to become a Marine:

> I do not know if it is right to do what God wants or what I want, which I have been taught is a sin... The only way that I think war can cause good is by spreading God's word. If I did go to war that is what I think God would want me to do: take a bad situation and make it into a good one.
>
>   At the end of this play, Brecht and I have ended up at the same conclusion, and that is that war is wrong. We both came to it in two very different ways, because he was not religious at all, but he and I are thinking the same way. Brecht knew what to do with this belief. He wrote *Mother Courage and Her Children* and used it as a way to show how bad war is. I do not know what to do.

When Jeremiah looked up, I told him, in front of the class, how incredible I thought his paper was.

I had received another equally unbelievable paper. Henry's paper opened:

> What would you say if I told you I could offer you a deal of a lifetime? This deal would set you up for the rest of your life. It would provide you a free education that would have otherwise cost you roughly $42,000 a year. It would pay for your books, your room and board, and on top would pay you a stipend of $300 a month. After you receive this free education after four years you will have a guaranteed job with a decent salary and loads of benefits—benefits that include free housing, free healthcare, and great insurance, among other things. This job will not only pay the bills and sup-

port your family, but it will also have you be known as a hero to your friends, family, and the rest of the country.

Now what if I told you that this same job had some side effects. This same job will mean you will be separated from your family for long periods of time. I mean, you will be sent overseas for months at a time and put in potentially very dangerous places. The experience from this job could haunt you forever and change who you are as a person. This job could cause you to lose not only your mind, but also arms, legs, feet, hands, and possibly your life. I am talking about the job of being an officer in the United States Army.

Henry had been the only student to compare himself to Mother Courage. 'I began to see,' he'd concluded, 'how both Mother Courage and I are profiting in some way from war.' That, I thought, was what I'd hoped Brecht might be able to do—force students to think about the choices they were making.

The essays I hadn't been expecting were about how Mother Courage was a strong figure who didn't cave, regardless. When I questioned these students, asking them if, really, they thought that the cost of losing her children for the sake of her cart was worth it, they answered, What was Mother Courage supposed to do, cry? No, she picked up and moved on, just like a soldier on the battlefield has to do if one of his brothers gets killed.

Percival put it this way: If...Mohamed Bouaziz, a fruit vendor from Tunisia, could sacrifice himself and change the lives of millions in North Africa, why couldn't Mother Courage sacrifice herself or lose her cart to save her children? I have pondered this question and have come up with one logical answer. What Mohamed Bouaziz did was to stand up and show what the oppression of a dictatorship does in Tunisia and, in doing so, caused a chain reaction of reform. However, had Mother Courage sacrificed herself to save her children, her children would have suffered more than she would have. Her sacrifice would have been pointless. Mother Courage was a businesswoman, and that is what she specialized in. If she were to lose her cart, then she couldn't feed her kids and they would probably die a horrible way in the war... Mohamed Bouaziz died and did a noble act, even if it was not intentional. Mother Courage allowed her children to die, but this seems more out of mercy than selfishness, because they didn't have to suffer any longer once they were dead.

Papers, like Percival's, heroizing Mother Courage made me think of the introduction to *Jarhead,* in which Anthony Swofford describes being at a base in California, waiting to deploy at the beginning of the first Iraq war, and drinking beer and watching war movies with his platoon buddies. They watch *Apocalypse Now*, *Platoon*, and *Full Metal Jacket* all the while yelling *Semper fi*, and getting off on 'the rape scenes when American soldiers return from the bush after killing many VC to sip cool beers in a thatch bar while whores sit on their laps...before they retire to rooms and fuck the whores sweetly.' Swofford posits that even though those movies might be called anti-war films, 'Vietnam war films are all pro-war, no matter what the supposed message, what Kubrick or Coppola or Stone intended. Filmic images of death and carnage are pornography for the military man; with film you are stroking his cock, tickling his balls with the pink feather of history, getting him ready for his real First Fuck.'

I was realizing, reading Brecht with cadets, that even an anti-war text could be read as a pro-war one. I was familiar with Sontag's argument that photographs could never serve an intended political agenda, that they could only 'give rise to opposing responses. A call for peace. A cry for revenge. Or simply the bemused awareness, continually restocked by photographic information, that terrible things happen.' So I shouldn't have been surprised by the fact texts were no different. But I was. What was the purpose of literature, I found myself asking. Yes, it often changed people's lives, but what did it really mean if the reader was always more powerful than the writer?

I had once studied under Swofford. I hadn't been keen on learning from him, but I had needed the class to fulfill degree requirements. One of his beginning assignments was to write a piece of erotic fiction. I had been so bothered by having been asked to write something of this nature for him, I had ended up trying on the voice of Private Steven Green. I had wanted to shock Swofford. I had wanted to write something utterly repugnant. I had wanted him to have to face who he was as he read my words.

Ultimately, I had wanted to give the person who had shred rhetoric in front of my eyes in his introduction to *Jarhead* porn that he couldn't enjoy.

Such attempts couldn't work—he had warned me. He never responded to my completed assignment. The piece itself had been a failure in its attempt to convince anyone of anything. However, I still vividly remember writing it, as I felt for those hours at the keyboard as if I had become Green, the white heat in which I was writing and the white heat in which Green had committed his unspeakable crimes in Iraq had, it seemed to me then, met and swirled.

~

I heard the news on my way to school. Had a reporter really said that we'd taken custody of Osama bin Laden's body and thrown it in the ocean? And the talk of a never-before-seen stealth helicopter, abandoned at bin Laden's Pakistani compound? Then, too, there was mixed-up reporting of the event itself—the story changing even as I listened.

You didn't hear? The cops came, people were throwing flares, one student informed me breathlessly, as soon as I entered the classroom.

Students had, I quickly learned, spent the night celebrating. 'Bin Laden's death causes campus party,' the student newspaper read. Fires had been started and fire alarms pulled in almost every campus building.

~

'We are a weird country. We think revenge is justice. We murder our friends and parade around with bloody hands, waving at crowds, blowing kisses,' I emailed my parents.

All of it was heinous. I couldn't contain my anger, but I had to. I took the studded tires off my truck and graded papers, like Lewis's titled 'Literature Will Never Die,' that read:

Theodor Adorno argues that after events such as the Holocaust and places like Auschwitz, literature could no longer exist... This belief is based on the premise that after atrocities people can simply no longer write the way they could before. But what if the effect of such atrocities does the exact opposite? It's not that atrocities end literature, they fuel literature. Without genocide and other atrocities around the world, people wouldn't have anything to write about. That is why these atrocities do not end poetry, as Adorno states, but rather these horrible events actually create and inspire authors to write literature.

Justification of war for the sake of literature! I hadn't expected it, but I knew that I, too, was wrestling this demonic question myself. Wasn't I being paid blood money to teach at a military college, and didn't I need conflict to fuel my own writing? Wasn't this, as Walter Benjamin once so succinctly stated, barbarism?

And then there were papers like Bev's. 'The main reason I decided to stay with the Army is because one day I hope to deploy with my mother,' she had written. 'Yes, I know that is wishful thinking and a little too perfect to imagine, but if I had the chance to deploy with my mother, there is not a thing I would not do in order to ensure her safety. She has three children, including myself, and I want her to come home safely to us.' Deploying with one's mother? It was a concept so foreign to me that I had to reread Bev's essay.

If Brecht had made Mother Courage a man, would the play have been as provocative? I had asked students earlier that term.

No! they had practically shouted. She had to be a mother.

Why? What did it mean to be a mother in this day and age?

A Short History of Our Flesh and Blood

Dear Candide,

Creation, be it virtual or metaphorical, strives to free us all. As James Baldwin put it: 'the war of an artist with his society is a lover's war, and he does, at his best, what lovers do, which is to reveal the beloved to himself, and with that revelation, make freedom real.' The history of adoption, however, speaks less of freedom than of its lack. Still, here are our present facts: I am a 39-year-old, single, North American woman, and my chances of having my own biological child at this late age are slim. You are one of 8.2 million orphans in the Democratic Republic of the Congo. In one of my favorite novels, *Maps*, by Nuruddin Farah, the protagonist, a Somali boy is adopted by an Ethiopian family servant after the death of his parents; later, he is sent to live with his biological Somali aunt and uncle in Mogadishu. Farah uses examples of nontraditional family structures to critique patriarchy and nationalist identity. I bring this book up, because I would like to see my adoption of you through such an emerald, liberatory lens. But I don't. In fact, despite all the joy I have experienced imagining you as my daughter, I can't see it that way.

Our circumstances disallow what might be identity-shattering anywhere else. After years of colonial terrors done unto your people, war continues to decimate your country and its environment. This war is primarily being fought for coltan, the mineral ore used in cell phone batteries, laptops, and playstations. Troops from Rwanda (known for putting an end to the genocide in Rwanda) started this conflict by pressing into eastern Congo and setting up camps in mining areas. At the peak of the technological boom in the late 1990s, the Rwandan Army was raking in $20 million a month from coltan mining. Three companies, at the time, bought this mineral ore—one was German, the other Chinese, and the third North American. To spell out what this means: as a North American, as a cell phone user, as a woman typing this letter to you on her laptop, I am, in part, to blame. Five million people have been killed in your country and an epidemic of rape and sexual mutilation has also broken out as a result of this conflict. Women have been and continue to be raped so violently they can no longer bear children. Many have become infected with HIV. Today AIDS-related illnesses are the leading cause of death for those between ages 20 and 49 in your country—one of 20 countries identified by the World Health Organization as having the highest unmet need for antiretroviral therapy. More than one-tenth of your country's population are orphans, and one in eight of these orphans have lost their parents to sicknesses associated with AIDS.

Here, in the U.S., AIDS kills a disproportionate amount of African Americans (a consequence, some argue, of urban renewal projects of the 1950s-70s, when large numbers of blacks were forced to leave their often poor, but socially strong inner city neighborhoods, and were scattered into outlying housing projects where they were socially ostracized, and increasingly suffered from loss of employment, turned to crack and prostitution, and started spreading the HIV virus). Perhaps the proliferation of unsafe sexual practices also affects the lower childlessness rates for women of color nearing forty years of age, as these rates aren't as high as the childless rates of white women of the same age. Still, according to the June fertility supplement of the Census Bureau's current population study, the childless rates for women of color are growing, and in the last twenty years, the number of *all* women in the United States over 35 having babies has nearly doubled. Many of these women pay tens of thousands of dollars to get pregnant using in vitro fertilization techniques. For older women, risks of such late pregnancies include a 1 in 70 chance of delivering a Down syndrome baby, and an inability to carry a child past the second trimester, but these risks are stared down; maternal desire is fierce. Economists are just now determining that the rates of childlessness are also proportionate to income (the more a woman makes, the less likely she will be to have children) and consumption. As one economist puts it, each statistically average North American now consumes energy at a rate sufficient to sustain a 66,000-pound primate and has offspring at the same slow rate predicted for a beast this size.

These are the realities against which my desire to mother you is set. At first, before I ever saw your picture on a website listing waiting children, I thought I would foster a child. This, I still believe, is the most ethical way to be matched with a child. Then I attended a foster meeting where I was told that in the state of Vermont I could expect to foster a teenage child and that this teen would not want to bond with me. I was told stories of foster children who set fire to foster parents' homes and stole from them. I was, at the time, newly out of a relationship in which I had been a pseudo-mother to my then partner's teenage daughter. Only as her father's and my relationship was ending, had this teenage girl begun to accept me. I didn't think that I could face that same scenario again, so I began to look into other options—one of which included surfing the net for sperm. Even had I somehow been able to bear the thought of a stranger impregnating me, I had no idea how to choose from among the numerous donors listed according to education, race, height, and weight. The disproportionate amount of white donors to donors of color and the absolute lack of any donor with dark listed under the category of skin color scared me. In the back of my mind, too, was the story of my friend's friend—a single, female professor who went through in vitro fertilization treatments and got pregnant, but shortly thereafter died swimming in a pool, the cause of her death related to blood clots caused by fertility medicines.

How to embrace this reproductive technology that grew out of women's rights struggles? Such struggles formed me. I remember wearing a shirt as a child with a logo that said: *a woman's place is in the house and the senate.* I also remember standing on a street corner, age twelve, with signs demanding my reproductive rights. Having a child, as I understood it then as a pre-teen, then later as a teen, and even throughout my twenties, would be the end of my independence; an independence others had fought to insure me, an independence my mother hadn't known, and that many women around the world might never know; an independence I have seen challenged again and again, most recently in the state of Mississippi where, had the vote passed, a proposed amendment to the state's constitution would have declared a fertilized egg a person, which would have rendered some birth control and in vitro fertilization techniques equivalent to murder.

Shulamith Firestone's once deemed radical position in *The Dialectic of Sex* that cloning would bring an end to the tyranny of biology, and that the end of the biological family would spell the cessation of the psychology of power is complicated, as my friend April points out, by the fact that even when children are removed from equations of male-female relations, women are, in large numbers, still abused by men. In direct opposition to Firestone's cloning call, Dr. Eleanora Porcu, inventor of the technology to freeze women's eggs, actually believes that freezing one's eggs to postpone childbearing is *harmful* to feminism. 'It means that we're accepting a mentality of efficiency in which pregnancy and motherhood are marginalized,' Porcu says. 'We've demonstrated that we are able to do everything like men. Now we have to do the second revolution, which is not to become dependent on a technology that involves surgical intervention. We have to be free to be pregnant when we are fertile and young.' What scares me isn't the gross violations many, particularly older women, may choose to take on, so as to become pregnant, it's the question of—should cloning or ectogenesis (the gestation of the fetus outside of the human body) be developed and enter the market—what kind of technologically birthed human beings might be mass produced. Eugenic thinking is always a threat. Just look at history: before we began applying reproductive technologies to humans, we applied them to plants and animals. Eugenics, as a concept, stems from the American Breeders' Association (for livestock) which formed the Eugenics Record Office in the early twentieth century, claiming that the most progressive revolution in history would take place as soon as selective breeding techniques for animals and plants were applied to human beings. The Eugenics Record Office's director foresaw a time when a woman wouldn't marry a man 'without knowing his biologico-genealogical history,' in the same way a stockbreeder would reject 'a sire for his colts or calves' who was without pedigree. What is already true of adoption (white families largely wanting white children) points to what might happen, should reproductive technologies remain in the hands of the current free market. But something perhaps equally frightening is happening today, and that is how U.S. reproductive desires (and, one might argue, lack of such technologies as cloning) are played out on other nations' women's children and wombs.

In the case of international adoption, women who die before their children are grown often come from countries like yours. Women like me wait eagerly to sweep in and rescue motherless children like you. And then there are the cases of women who are no longer fertile and want a biological child, not to mention single or coupled gay men who want the same, and seek out cheap wombs to inseminate. India boasts one of the fastest, largely unregulated, and growing rent-a-womb industries. Hundreds of foreign tourists are said to travel there each year to hire women to incubate their children. In 2002, the country legalized commercial surrogacy to promote medical tourism. This tourism is predicted to generate $2.3 billion annually by next year. The entire process costs customers around $23,000, less than one-fifth of what is charged in the U.S. In North America, medical professionals are advised to only implant one embryo in a woman's uterus per attempt, but in India, some professionals routinely implant five at a time, aborting anything more than two fetuses. Indian women routinely risk their lives for the $7,500 payment each receives for delivering someone else's child.

Looking closely at this situation, the divide between first and third world feminisms is rendered painfully acute. What are women's rights? I will leave this question hanging, as an unparalleled catastrophic reality awaits us. This October, the world's population hit seven billion. Only if the human population stabilizes at eight to 12 billion, can we continue to bear two children per family. Otherwise we're doomed—the earth's ecosystem will collapse. This kind of takes the air out of this whole reproductive affair, shouldn't it? But nothing is as simple as rational thought, and nothing is as difficult. It is in the face of all this history and information that I write to you, and what do you want of such mumbo-jumbo? You are a child. You deserve to dream, not to be cautioned by apocalyptic tales. And yet, you are living an apocalyptic tale yourself. There are 16 million AIDS orphans in the world; of these, 14.8 million live where you do, in sub-Saharan Africa. Had these orphans' parents been granted access to antiretroviral therapies, orphans like you would still be living at home, rather than in institutions, on the streets, with surrogate families, and in other countries.

Last month in a *New York Times* opinion article Drucilla Cornell raised the issue of international adoption generally being a one-way street from the Global South to the Global North, and conceded that often those who adopt children from the Global South are hailed as saviors of children from countries that have fallen into hell, on the grounds that those children were unlikely to grow up to lead meaningful lives, or even to physically survive. This humanitarian gesture, Cornell argued, is problematic, because it also engenders in the adopted child a traumatic break from her homeland. Cornell, who adopted her daughter from Paraguay, said she enabled her daughter's life by adopting her, but in another sense violated her

by uprooting her. This op-ed caused a flurry of responses, all of which cir-
cled issues of nationality and birth culture, monetary privilege and the lack
thereof, and the question of whether the trauma of international adoption
was, indeed, ethical and/or worth it. I read the article and the responses
with my heart in my throat.

Kurt in New York responded to Cornell's op-ed with vitriol, questioning the idea of a child as being a national of anywhere:

> Adopting a foreign child is an enabling violation? As an adoptive
> father of three children from Korea, I greatly resent the oh-so-su-
> perior elitist garbage passing for thought here. A child needs par-
> ents. Period. A child is not plural as in all children of any society.
> A child is neither black or white or Latino or Asian. A child is not
> an avatar of on[e] group of suffering humanity. A child is an indi-
> vidual human being with specific needs... [W]ould the intellectual
> opinion artist pushing this guilt trip feel the child would be better
> being warehoused with dozens of others in factory-like orphanag-
> es? Well, at least their caretakers (when they see them) will talk to
> them in their own language, huh? By the way, what is a child's own
> language? What is his native culture?

Kurt's attack on Cornell's intellectualism smacked up against my own need
to attempt to understand our situation. Cornell, in my opinion, wasn't even
probing these issues of inequality and identity very deeply. But reading
Kurt's comment, I could not help but think of you, a six-year-old, already
cognizant of your nationality and race, and fluent in your native tongue.
Children all do come from somewhere; white people have tried to am-
putate persons of color from their roots for centuries. Nonetheless, Kurt's
emotional insistence that a 'child is a child,' kept tugging at me. Part of
me wanted to be able to think so purely, to forget all contexts, and embrace the justifications for international adoption that people like Kurt or
Anne, from Ridgefield, Connecticut, had. 'Please spend some significant
time hanging out in an orphanage in the developing world, observing the
poor nutrition, primitive medical care, lack of stimulation, and lack of direct *contact comfort* that all children need for normal development. It will
make you cry,' Anne's post read. 'Then come back and talk to me about the
philosophical value of *birth culture*. Yes, in the perfect world, a child would
not have to face the identity issues that adopted kids have to face.'

I did spend time in an orphanage in the developing world. I went, in 2006, to Rwanda to build a school for orphans of the genocide. This experience didn't justify anything; I only became hungrier to figure out sustainable responses to economic inequalities and racial, ethnic, gender-based, and religious hate as a result. How blind people can be in their assumptions that the third world orphan in question will always be better off with a North American family! I had no such faith when I began adopting you—and not because I didn't think I would be a good mother. Despite this, however, I was hopeful in a way that made me no different than Kurt or Anne, or from any of the adoptive parents with whom I was emailing at that time who sang their adopted children's praises. In one such message, I was told of a Congolese child, who, when his adoptive parents had gone to get him, had been so hungry he screamed if he wasn't being fed; once he knew there was food readily available, he had to eat all the time.

I thought, as I mailed the $712 to the agency to secure my match with you and to pay for your blood test, that I was someone who could at the very least feed you. But as I sent off the check and paperwork, another part of me was cognizant that a multitude of horrors had had to happen to enable me to adopt you. I knew about these injustices as they circled your country and mine, but I didn't want to apply what I knew to you and me. I just kept looking at your photograph in which you stand so thin up against an orphanage wall, your name masking taped to your T-shirt: 'Candide.'

I had turned to international adoption, as it, in comparison to other options, seemed cheaper, easier, faster, and possible for a single woman like me, and the Congo, in particular, had the least restrictive of all adoption policies. I had inquired, before seeing your photograph, about a Chinese baby, only to be informed that I had to have $100,000 in assets in order to even qualify for adopting from China. And then, when I was told that I could go ahead and adopt you, I knew only that you were thought to be in good health. I wanted to believe it was okay to desire to mother you. When I received the call a week later, telling me that your blood tests had come back positive for HIV, I thought that the agency was calling to tell me that my financial situation was not adequate; I had braced myself for disappointment—thinking the financial strain would be the hardest part of the initial process. I cradled the phone. I'm so sorry, the woman at the agency said.

After I was given this information, I began to imagine that my adopting you would promise you a longer life by giving you access to antiretroviral therapy. I felt a purpose and less consumed with guilt for engaging in transnationally adopting a child. That could be really meaningful, was my friend John's response when I told him what I was doing.

After I had had time to mourn, after I had had time to grow scared, after I had had time to research what it would mean to continue with your adoption, and after I had decided that I would do this if my visiting professorship was converted into a tenure-line position as I was almost convinced it would be, I began to see *myself* as living with HIV. I knew, of course, that my identification with you was as ridiculous as one of the comments I had read online in response to Cornell's op-ed in which an adoptive father, Mark E. White, wrote in to say that after adopting two daughters from Ethiopia, he felt the entire family had become Ethiopian-American. The post had stunned me. For one, I didn't believe such cultural differences could be so easily integrated. It was true, I imagined, that White's identity had shifted after the adoption of his girls, but how could he claim to be Ethiopian-American?

Today, there is a growing movement of persons in the U.S. who feel it necessary to author their own gender pronouns, as well as their own racial pronouns. These choices, like my own choice to identify with you, however, remain choices only for the privileged. And choosing to be female, for instance, when one is biologically male, might also, in the short run, severely hamper women's solidarity movements, even as they aid queer movements. Such identity choices run the risk of granting more power to the already powerful, in an attempt to liberate a few, in a society that sees race first and foremost as skin tone (then by ethnic and cultural affiliations, and lastly by what one does/performs) and likewise sees gender as a biologically sealed deal. Similarly, identifying with and choosing to adopt positive children internationally is a band-aid, offering a select few children medical care and sometimes loving parents. I wonder if the rate of international adoption of sick children increases, whether the lack of systemic change in poor countries will also increase. What, in other words, is really happening? Sure, it might look like a radical act for a white, North American parent to mother a black African child, but to translate such privilege into global terms: the more the first world gets what it wants on the whole, the more the rest of the world suffers.

It seems, then, important to articulate that international adoption is a very pertinent definition of neocolonialism. This is what the world has come to: the slow death of those formerly and ongoingly enslaved and denied. Some international adoptees, according to Mirah Riben, even compare being adopted to slavery. Jane Jeong Trenka and Tobias Hubinette speak out about feeling like strangers in both worlds: not American and no longer Asian or Latina, unable to speak the language of their families when, as adults, they struggled to reunify. What is at stake, even given the exceptions—those, for instance, who argue that love is thicker than blood (and how I yearn for us to be among such exceptions)—is a globalized reproductive industry in which the rich exploit and enslave the poor for their bodily services and kin.

So, you might ask, knowing what I know, knowing that the baby industry is worse than crooked, knowing even that the agency I was using was once involved in a trafficking incident in the Marshall Islands, how could I have continued the process of adopting you? I don't know. For one, you were sick and I assumed you needed medical help. Secondly, I already cared about you. Then, too, there is my own almost excusable situation. After I had begun to adopt you, and my father was trying to talk me out of it, I voiced to him that his and my mother's loss of a child (who had trouble breathing and died in my mother's arms just a month before I was born) had cemented something inside me, as if preventing me from birthing a child of my own. (It was after this loss that my parents themselves thought of adopting a Vietnamese child fathered by an African-American G.I., but when they were told no one could guarantee that the child would arrive in the U.S. healthy or even alive, they knew they couldn't do this. I was raised an only child. Curious as to what sibling I might have had, I read of the Amerasian adoptions that commenced in the spring of 1975, as Saigon fell to Communist troops and rumors spread that southerners associated with the U.S. might be massacred. The evacuation of 2,000 war orphans—not all of whom were orphans, as, in the haste to evacuate, documentation was sometimes inaccurate—was tragic: Operation Babylift's first official flight crashed outside of Saigon, killing 144 people, most of them children.)

Then, months into the process of adopting you, I was told that my job would not be converted to a tenure-line one and that I was no longer guaranteed health insurance. A kind of chord in my heart popped. 'Come get me a net, gather me up, because I am no longer alive,' I wrote in my journal. 'Go fetch. Never bring it back to me. What ache did I paddle? So I am colder now. So I am hurt. So everything just careens around me. Broken hoops. Horseshoes. Treads of mud. You airlifted me; you sent me back.' When I wrote that I must have been thinking of Fanny Howe's short story, 'The Weather,' of the white couple who adopt a black boy and then can't deal with the decision they made, which is the racial crisis they are living, and so give the boy back to the agency from which he came. Or perhaps I was thinking of the parents who, a year ago, put a child they had adopted from Russia onto an airplane and flew the child back alone.

Some people have described the wretched conditions of orphanages in the Congo and the lack of light in children's eyes. I was told, however, that the orphanage in which you are housed is better than most. I recently spoke with our former adoption agency; they have decided not to continue to work with your orphanage. They said those who run your orphanage lied to their agency, telling them that several children, like you, were healthy, and then turned around and said that you weren't. This was after the agency gave your orphanage a significant amount of money to enable adoptions.

Desperation, be it caused by poverty or another kind of hunger, does horrible things to all parties. I thought that you weren't being treated with antiretroviral therapy, though perhaps you are. Or maybe (if it is true that those who run the orphanage are lying and not the agency staff, who wouldn't give me the name of your orphanage) you are not positive at all. If you are positive, and are being treated, then you are between the two and 24 percent of the positive population in the Congo that I've read who are. Which percentage is it? Two or 24? I read somewhere else, too, that there is only one pediatric hospital in all of the DRC for kids with AIDS. But a woman who adopted a positive child through the same agency I was using, albeit from a different Congolese orphanage than yours, recently told me that her son was treated with antiretroviral meds while at his orphanage. She hadn't known, and had specifically asked that he not be started on such medications before his adoption, as she wanted to make sure, she said, he was compliant and didn't become resistant to the therapy, which can happen if the medicine isn't administered properly. When she arrived in the Congo, however, she learned that her son had been on the therapy for two years. He had been very sick when he had arrived at the orphanage and they had started him on the meds then. The orphanage had been very serious about giving him his doses at the necessary times, and his health was, as a result, very good. She was, she said, 'quite impressed with what they have there—chewable pills that include a cocktail of three meds. They were,' in her words, 'much more convenient than what we have here!'

Who should I thank for putting their lives on the line so that that medicine is made available at reasonable costs to people like this woman's son and, perhaps, to you—and to the other (if one believes the higher stats) quarter of the two million positive persons in your country? I know a few names, Zackie Achmat and Paul Farmer among them. There must be more. I need to thank them. But really, I need to do more, for what does sitting in my apartment alone, typing this letter to you do? I am asking you. I would like to know what you think. I do not know how to free us. Right now, I'm reading an interview with South African author Sindiwe Magona. She speaks of AIDS as genocide. She says men and women must stand up and say that they won't die or kill another because of sex. She speaks of the apartheid conditions that caused men to leave their families to find work elsewhere, and how this engendered the now present non-loyal paternal attitude. Playboys, she says, should be called murderers. Women, she even offers, might be better off 'turning lesbian' than marrying unfaithful men and dying of AIDS. But behavior isn't all that needs to change; systems and governments and markets must.

You are so much more than your illness or race or nationality, but these are the dominating markers that society assigns, and which we must wrestle, trying to find our individuality amid the blinders of labels and social mores. I, too, hope that I am more than the slew of research I fling at you... And if you aren't being treated and you are sick? Then you are dying. This possibility is the one I don't know how to bear.

In an old letter to you, I wrote: 'I want to wake you and carry you into the forest. I want to show you the woods. I want to bury your hands in moss.' I remember writing this after my six-year-old neighbor Trey and I spent the afternoon in the forest building fairy houses. We used a broken mushroom for a sofa, and I talked about mushrooms. I told Trey that they were alive and not to kick them. I said, Maybe the mushrooms hear us talking about them.

But Trey was adamant: Mushrooms don't have ears!

Maybe they do and we don't know, I said.

Yeah, maybe they're under the ground, Trey agreed.

We were quiet because we didn't want to offend any mushroom. We sat down on a bench and Trey asked, Are there any mushrooms around here?

I looked. We eventually saw some. We didn't talk about them and smiled.

I had imagined sitting on that bench with you.

Now, all I see when I think of you are images of women surrogates in India; containers for babies. Is *The Handmaid's Tale* coming true? What are our fictions? And what is happening to the world? To other women's bodies? Our own? What is our hunger? Tragic—the circumstances as I write these words to you.

P.S.

What is this poetic practice, this letter to you? I would say it represents what words can and cannot do. Words cannot mend everything. They could not save, for instance, the relation between poets Paul Celan and Ingeborg Bachmann. Their letters to one another—some of the most powerful were never sent—still burn across a divide too great for us all. Celan and Bachmann lived together once, then parted, then met up again, then parted, then met up again, and so on. 'Lamp-searchingly,' is how Celan signed one of his letters to Bachmann; he, a man who had survived a labor camp and the murder of his parents and had become a poet, was coming to visit her, a woman who had survived being born into a National Socialist family and had, too, emerged a poet. They were respectively a Jewish poet and a female poet at a time when these identities were weighted. She was moving into a new apartment and he wrote that he would help her find a lamp. Soon their affair would end; neither could save the other. Celan would break down and ultimately kill himself, and Bachmann would burn to death in a house fire.

So many instances of global divides, so many instances of tortured love, and in the face of it all, how does one go on? Lamp-searchingly?

A few weeks ago, I walked through long grasses with my friend Amos, together with his mother, his sister's wife, and his sister's and sister's wife's daughter (born from his sister's harvested egg, sperm from a donor, and carried to term by his sister's wife). I could hear the rush of grasses. We walked through a field, mountains in the distance, the sky darkening, with children swinging their mason-jar-and-tea-light-lanterns that they had decorated with color tissue paper. My friend's niece held her lantern by its copper wire handle. She was excited to see a boy who had flat eyes and blond highlighted hair and who couldn't keep his hands to himself. I watched him try to steal a small girl from another girl's arms. Ages three and four, all of them. Behind us, a girl with bangs started to talk. She has a crush on me, the girl was saying, speaking of the child with whom I was walking over uneven ground, a child who likes carrots and dinosaurs and climbing up onto surfaces of tables and swings. She also likes to sing. It's disgusting, she's always hugging me, the other girl went on.

This girl's mother said nothing. One mother of the child I was with quickly intervened and pointed to the moon.

Are you looking up, Candide?

Twenty-six gallons of water was recently found on the moon. How many ways are there of fertilizing? How much life is there beyond our imagining? What is a lantern walk in a field of children?

I look out the window. It is black. Is there electricity, or are there lamps, or candles at your orphanage?

A Short History of Revolution

Rose, red like a flag
—a revolution.

A child.
A child.

—Forough Farrokhzad

Here in the chair that smells of someone else's perfume, here in the chair that I dragged up from beside the dumpster that is perennially too full, the dumpster children play near, the dumpster behind which my neighbor, age seven, told me someone had been killed by an army of skunks (she also said that she had the wild cough—a cough that wouldn't hurt a person, but was contagious to animals), I sit and write to you, Forough Farrokhzad, poet of poets, who went against the bounds of time and place and chose sin for its truth.

Last night I read your poem 'Let Us Believe in the Beginning of a Cold Season' out loud to my dog. I was naked in the bathtub. My dog stood over me. I had filled the bath, because the apartment was too cold, I was too cold, and you—you were cold in the poem and naked: 'I am naked, naked, naked / naked like the moments of silence between the phrases of love / And my wounds are all due to love / from love, love, love.'

My dog stood over me, listening to the odd words streaming from my mouth. Her ears tilted up, her jowls hung over the lip of the tub. She lapped some water, left, came back. I slipped more deeply into the bath water. 'Why do you always keep me at the bottom of the sea?' Reading your poem, I became your voice and felt washed by its cadence. I thought, as I bathed, of the child of lepers you adopted and what he said, later, when interviewed as an adult, about your voice: it rendered him speechless.

You held his hand on the train. You hold my hand. I am not on a train. I am not a six-year-old child. But I can imagine you with him—a child you mothered in place of the child who was forbidden contact with you after you left your marriage. Forough, you show me how a single woman can buck the system, live her life out loud.

Once, in India, a pregnant leper serenaded me, her fingerless hands begging. The boy you adopted would have become a leper, too. In the film you made of the leper colony, he runs to get his father his crutches. It is the poignancy of this boy's need to please, his love, his prescient knowing that you will spirit him away and that he is unable to do anything about it, that mends your heart. Before you adopted this boy, you would cry, your mother says, the whole night, every night.

The child you adopted is now a man who wrestles your poems into another language. There is a grace to him, just as there is a force that keeps propelling him toward you. He opens a store door. He reads your poems out loud to the store's owner. You crashed your car and died when he was nine.

I take out my pen and write a letter.

Your adopted son writes back.

A Short History of Reluctant Fundamentalism

In Lahore, Pakistan, Naveed and I talk of Yannis Ritsos. Naveed mentions the homosocial appearing in Ritsos's poems. I hadn't seen it there before. Did you know, I ask Naveed, Ritsos painted on pebbles?

At the park: trees with Islamic verses tacked to their trunks. At one time these signs, Naveed says, denoted the trees' species. Do you see what's become of us?

We sit on the hillside under a tree, smoking in the odd evening chill. A beggar woman comes and sits in front of us, saying her arm doesn't work. Naveed responds calmly, sweetly.

After she leaves, he tells me that his father called him a sisterfucker, so he turned around and called his father a motherfucker. His mother told him to run. He ran, scaled the wall, and had to stay away for a week, his father shooting his gun after him.

~

Ancient rooms on top of rooms framed by wood, like in *Battle of Algiers*. An old brothel. The giant mosque next door built in the 17th century. We eat while looking out upon it. A kind of grace? The sadness of who we are on the top floor of such a place. Traffic. Children in cars. One child with hands pressed against the glass.

~

I recognize the balcony at Naveed's from a place I once stayed outside Kathmandu. Naveed's apartment, too, feels familiar. I live alone and somewhat sparsely like this. Jars of nuts—cashews, almonds in front of us, as we continue speaking in the dark.

~

Moshin Hamid's *The Reluctant Fundamentalist* is a beautiful, yet calculatingly cool book. Its title does not serve; the main character is not reluctant and not a fundamentalist. Nor does the ending particularly help—both title and ending are cheap; the real story is elsewhere. I am interested in Hamid's treatment of sexuality and politics. His fiction is marketed as political, but sex remains its centerpiece. Like Daniyal Mueenuddin's *In Other Rooms, Other Wonders*, Hamid's tone is distanced—from the women characters, especially. Mueenuddin's writing is grim, even cruel. He has been called a reluctant feudalist for inscribing a particularly—and not necessarily realistic—feudal order onto all the women in his stories. Hamid is not much better.

~

Pomegranate buds inlaid in white marble. Naveed tells me of Noor Jehan, jealous wife of King Jahangir, both buried in this garden. Was it she who covered Jahangir's tomb in such obscenely beautiful lapis lazuli blossoms—the very bud after which he named his true love, Anarkali? Anarkali danced for him when he was still a prince. She was but a maid and Jahangir's father ordered her buried alive. Some theorize Jahangir built tunnels for her escape. Others say Anarkali was a Hindu boy.

    Naveed leads me to Jahangir's blossomed tomb, and tells me, pointing to the colorful stone, that he would have this bud for a tattoo. Behind us, in the garden, men sip soda through long straws. Children toss giant balloons. One of the dead in Afghanistan today: a child wearing red pajamas. What has happened that an American soldier can leave an outpost, walk down a dark road, and shoot and stab 17 persons, nine of them children? I see loneliness amidst a crowd, as if sitting by itself on a fallen tree. Leaves crackle. Naveed laughs at a boy with a scar crossing his nose and then hands him several rupees. Two girls recognize in me a place they don't remember; one of them was born in Washington, D.C.

~

The university stands on a dusty patch of ground, concrete buildings bare, open to the wind. Women faculty outnumber men. The women are loud. Brimming, Naveed says, with sexual energy.

We are all honey in a sticky pot. I ask everyone to write down their formative experiences. Anjoo shares hers. She didn't want to marry, she says, and always wore jeans.

Her green eyes are set apart. She speaks of her mother and sister finding the right man for her after years of searching and of how she was afraid to go meet him, in case she might act too excited and her mother then call it off. The marriage was indeed arranged; she has been married for two months and is so happy. She admits to sensing a flicker of her father (who passed away five years ago) in this man. She can rely on him. He is solid, nothing riles him, she tells us. She is dressed in a pink sari and, when someone asks if she is on a diet now that she is married, she says, No!

~

A cab of women. Aneera talks of a book about a Saudi princess who leaves her husband when he tries to marry again; he wants more children and she has ovarian cancer. The princess flees, calls him from a country that she then leaves, making it impossible for him to trace her. When he finds out where she is and comes to retrieve her, she has the police ready to apprehend him. The story (based on fact) ends when the princess's cancer is cured, her husband takes her back, and she has another child. Maryam, who sits up front, is pregnant with her second child. It's her fifth pregnancy. Rida, a beautiful, smart woman in glasses, tells us of a tale in which a woman slaps her father. I am reminded of a film in which a girl trains as a boxer and knocks out her drunken father. We say we need these texts.

Do men, Maryam wants to know, stare at you here?

I haven't felt stared at, I say, but I've been with Naveed.

Maryam calls Naveed 'pure.'

I tell them of a woman screaming in the hotel room next door to mine, waking me at four in the morning.

The man is taking out his frustration on her sexually, Maryam responds, and then jokes about turning lesbian, her vibrator failing—these are, she says, her husband's threats when she grows mad at him.

~

I mistake the screen in Naveed's apartment for a fluorescent light. He flips a switch and the screen lowers. I have seen the projector hanging from the ceiling, but have not registered the fact that it is a projector. We've been smoking hash. Naveed's thumbnails are the thinnest crescents. His shoelaces are red. Watching Dryer's *Joan D'Arc*, I am conscious that I am reading her passion as sexual. As she suffers, as the flames lick her, I sense rapture. Naveed serves me tea with lemon rind.

Hours ago, he was rolling down the window, bargaining for flower wrist cuffs. He had told me to wear them. Will you wear one? I had asked.

I have, Naveed had said, I'm into gender bending.

Roses and daisies on wire, the cuffs make me happy. They are lavish.

What is it about Naveed's silence on the one hand and his frankness on the other that disarms me? He is my height, his goatee partly white. He lives in a concrete flat. Guards with guns patrol the entrance. Night folds over us. His wicker chairs corner me. He sleeps sometimes with boys he rents from the middle of the highway, boys who don't know what safe sex is. He teaches them.

~

The boy sits on the cart like he has sat there his whole life, as if an old man, but he is young—maybe four. His hands are cupped over his ears. The traffic is loud. I am inside a car. I have a driver. I am thinking of all those drivers killed while driving Americans through war zones. What does it mean, my sitting in this backseat, as we pass by boys playing billiards on outdoor tables, men squatting in front of fenced-in houses, graffiti, goats, fancy cars?

Last night, interviewing Naveed in his home about his work as a poet, I was as comfortable as (or even more comfortable than) I am in my own home. How odd, I told him, to feel so comfortable. What did you think you'd feel? he asked.

We ate beet soup under his Krishna paintings, laughing about his finding in Polish poetry something with which he identifies. Here, there is the beauty of feeling alive and understood, and the beauty of generosity and promise, when everything back home feels so hard, my father so sick, my life so solitary. But one cannot be a visitor forever. The boy on the donkey cart is no one I know. I will have to face the end of my family; I will have to envision life beyond.

~

Students aren't shocked at the opium eater being elected judge of the travelers. I've read John Berger's essay, 'Two Men Wrestling on a Sidewalk,' so many times, and finally, here in Lahore, it has a home—this tale of one boy's experience leaving India directly after Partition, and becoming one of the group of travelers led by a former addict. The boy's mother writes to him: 'My boy, in this life we are sometimes forced to eat shit. If this happens, eat as you've been brought up to eat, and wash your hands afterwards.'

~

I tell Naveed of my favorite student, Saqlain, who brought me another poem he had written, hoping that I might copy it, too, down in my notebook. Naveed's mind is elsewhere. He parks his small black car by a cemetery. We smoke hash at the foot of a dirt grave. Bats fly around us. Dried flowers hang on a string on the graveyard's iron. I think of the slow days ahead—my father really ailing. I try explaining to Naveed how tied up my identity is with my parents, not to mention with the house they built in which everything is a product of their own hands.

~

A girl beats soap into the fabric of a man's pants; she beats without effort, her whole body expert at such chores, the soap never splashing up, the rhythm of her stick steady, neither fast nor slow. The river is barely a river, more like a trickle, a thread of grey, a swamp-turned-cesspool. She soaps, beats, rinses, twists. Meanwhile, boys bother her. Her hair is tied back in a loose ponytail, her orange clothes light and airy. She is seven, has never been to school. She lives in a field with water buffalo and shares their curious eyes. Far away, my father tries to ready his own house for his decline, his hands swollen from carving a railing.

~

Naveed likes sunflowers (the only representation allowed in mosques) and writes in English, wishing for a written mother tongue. I watch the Urdu movie *Bol*. It is provocative; an indictment of male-dominated Pakistani life. My experience here is other than this. Fortress of feminism, Maryam calls the female faculty. *Bol* partially takes place in the red light district, highlights queens who paint trucks and one man's mania for a male child. After dinner, Hussnain stays late to speak to me of sexuality—curious, really curious, he says. The next day Naveed tells me that Hussnain is texting him love verses.

~

In *The Reluctant Fundamentalist*, a Pakistani, dazzled by all America has to offer him after his graduation from an Ivy League school, feels no pity for those killed on 9/11. After 9/11, his consciousness remains split. Similarly, it was in the cry for revenge that gripped the nation following 9/11 that I realized I could write nothing that wasn't concerned with my own anger. I—very much like Hamid's protagonist who returns to Pakistan to teach—am here in Lahore teaching today. In fact, my reality is such that I am sitting at a table with a Pakistani poet and teacher. Naveed and I utterly fit the roles of Hamid's protagonist and the American tourist to whom the protagonist tells his story—except that we've reversed the roles we're supposed to be playing. Naveed is asking about an essay I wrote about Saddam Hussein's hanging, in which I call attention to the execution as an injustice, naming it an act of neocolonial racism. Naveed is accusing me of making a martyr out of Hussein. I'm not exactly trying to make a martyr out of Hussein, I say. I'm simply trying to state how wrong my own nation's actions are by exploiting our persecution of one of the most indefensible tyrants.

As it is, *The Reluctant Fundamentalist* ends without resolution. No one quite understands the relation between the narrator and the tourist; they are linked together in a dangerous—or is it a tender?—dance, when the lights go out.

An Era of the American Taliban

My feet are cold, the barn loft drafty. I would be warm in Lahore. I would most certainly be in your kitchen, Naveed, drinking Lipton tea with lemon rind cut by that maid who broke your Buddha and made you upset with her questions about where the other foreign woman was and why I was in your flat. I felt faint jealousy for this European woman who had also stayed briefly with you. I knew her only through your maid and your one poem about the fern that prickled, like her skin, in the heat.

Had we met earlier, had we not been so wounded by our pasts, you with your two North American ex-wives, and me, a girl who once loved and lived for some time with a queer Spaniard, who would we have become? I am glad we met when we did. I am glad that you—at the very moment you were set to hire me—left the University of Management and Technology in Lahore and took another job. Better for you who had to hide your sexuality among the Muslim body at UMT, better for you who frequent Hindi temples dedicated to a saint and his younger male lover. (Did I tell you that I dreamed of Shah Hussain's mustard yellow' body? The dream was so *charged*.) I am glad, because even had I wanted to (and I did), I couldn't have run away to Pakistan and left my father to die alone. I thought perhaps that you would understand, but you had escaped from your parents when you came to study in the U.S., returning to Pakistan only after they passed. It took washing your father's body for you to begin to make your stilted peace, you, a queer son in a country that outlaws such sex.

When we met, you were apprenticing in the underground. It was beautiful to walk with you past the markered marble shrine: 'Call me for a good time.' Your profile on Manjam attracted the boy you referred to as your merman. Slim, pictured in a tunic, legs bare. 'I would swim across the Indian Ocean for you,' you wrote, texting him your photo with Pakistan's northern mountains behind you.

I can still see the queen in the middle of Lahore, his lipstick and exaggerated walk across the highway. The driver rolled up the window. The queen was left gesticulating, red-mouthed. The driver later asked me for money; his wife's mother was sick. I wanted you to give him the purse your former department gifted me, but we accidentally left it and the joint you gave me that I didn't smoke on my hotel bed, remember? We were on the way to the airport. In my backpack, I was carrying my favorite student Salman's poem about bin Laden that he had let me copy into my notebook:

> I don't know what is happening.
> The twin tower has been destroyed.
> The soldiers attacked the happy land.
> They wanted to find the hiding man.
> For that they forget the respect of the man.
> They searched Tarabara, Mijar and Kabul,
> but they still are hopeless. The drones
> are killing the innocents. There is rumor
> that they have found him in Abbottobad.

My notebook rested up against your book, *A Queen of No Ordinary Realms*.

You know, it was your poem about John Walker Lindh that permitted me entry to Pakistan. I read it in bed on one of those rare Vermont winter mornings when the sun was out. Like Lindh, I once read the Black Panthers, grew militant, dreamt of Afghanistan. I could easily have found my way there. In your poem, bearded grandmas see through Lindh's romantic ideas. He'll grow out of it, they predict. The poem itself predicts that sooner or later Lindh will find a new religion or war or both and that his semen-stained scarves, his masturbatory tools (the tools, you write, of a man who reads too much and makes no love) 'need to be buried or burned, lest they serve/as a noose for...notorious romantics.'

If I listen carefully, I can hear Salman's bin Laden whispering to your disheveled American, shot in the thigh, naked body duct-taped.

When I lived with my queer lover Luis, certain books took hold: Baldwin's *Giovanni's Room*; Verghese's *My Own Country*; Als' *The Women*. There was one night I remember above others, when I, slightly drunk, rode my bicycle through the dark on fire after having read Jean Genet's 'What Remains of a Rembrandt Torn into Little Squares All the Same Size and Shot Down the Toilet.' That was writing! That was the ultimate pulse! In this essay that's bifurcated until one side symbolically penetrates the other, Genet writes about flesh and its discontents. It is an essay on seeing another as one's self, and in this recognition comes repulsion so wretched (as wretched as Rembrandt's painted laugh is sad) that Genet can only imagine a future in which he can never love again. 'How to ignore,' he writes, '...that every attractive form, if it encloses me, is myself?'

When Luis and I met, I told him that I had already loved someone so completely that I could die happily. He said: The problem, Spring, is that you're a woman.

I liked Luis's company. Yes, he drove me mad; that was part of his charm. It was after he moved in and after he grabbed my hand one day while we were walking in the desert and asked why we never talked about our future together (in other words, after there was a seriousness to our relationship, despite the fact I was a woman) that the Abu Ghraib scandal broke. All world events originate, as you know, from within the domestic sphere. I taped the Abu Ghraib photographs to our apartment walls, tracing their iconography to other photographs, paintings, reading into the images, attempting to understand the impossible. Examining the photographs' confluence of torture and pornography, I considered Luis's foot on my nakedness. He wanted, he said, to walk on me. Where, I wanted to know, was the line between my lover's foot and the military torturer with his hoods and electrodes?

While still with Luis, I jotted the following down in my notebook:
Genet says that artists are one against a system and he identifies with criminals as they are against a system, too. He is against the state, against needing to justify the state, and is skeptical, as well, of the state-approved Left. Genet is beyond the Left. He's more radical. 'The very concern,' he writes, 'with creating a harmonious sentence supposes a morality; that is a relation between the author and possible reader.' Genet is against morals, like Badiou is against ethics. They impede growth, impede life, but no artist can be completely free of them. Genet remembers, however, writing in his cell—a place where he could write whatever he wanted and where he didn't imagine a readership. 'How do Maids,' he asks, 'speak to you in your heart?'

In Genet's only film, *Un Chant D'Amour*, a prison guard peeps through eyepieces mounted on the prisoners' doors and observes each prisoner masturbating. Although the guard enters one cell, whips a prisoner with his belt, and forces his pistol into the prisoner's mouth, his power is undermined by the prisoners' erotic reveries that free them momentarily from the confines of their cells and his furious watch. Desire, regulated by law, blooms in spite of everything, and sometimes—even if only fantastically—overcomes it all. In the film, two prisoners share the most erotic smoke through a hole in the wall.

On a related note, have you seen the video, Naveed, of Honey Boo Boo Child and her family eating outside? Beethoven's *Ode to Joy* plays. Shot in slow-motion, the video is nothing other than a family of fat North Americans enjoying a seemingly never-ending meal. It is the North American answer to Genet's *Chant*. It is the lowest of low art. It is pornography. This televised family eats what any supermarket in any town in this country supplies: cheap, addictive food. They eat outside. A fly flies by. I can remember being part of a family, eating hot dogs on the shore of Lake Iroquois—a small land-locked lake stolen from the Abenaki. The unbearability of this hunger makes me cry. Yet the way the entire family enjoys their meal! Has the slow motion made the repulsive enjoyable? Has the light? Rembrandt, where you at? Beethoven for dessert? Does it make me jealous, this family enjoying their instameal? I rarely eat with anyone else. I cook broccoli alone, bake a loaf of bread. Cook up miso soup. Sauté spinach with garlic. Drink tea. Not sweet ice tea, but pu-erh from China that's sold in a fermented brick. Call me classist tonight, but what makes this video of a reality TV child star about whom everyone complains because her mother enters her in pageants, feeds her energy drinks, and worries that she'll grow too thin for her own show, the bomb?

Stars generally make me want to vomit, but particularly child stars (even if I do love B-Girl Terra). I don't want kids to have to become anything other than kids. Some kids are out there working in mines, scrounging for e-waste, and being literally offed in classrooms, and child stars make me sick? I am talking, I suppose, of the world of prostitution—the prostitution of the image, a nation in which everything is done for money, everything is done for show. Honey Boo Boo, I've read, was discovered by Authentic Entertainment. The TLC network website taunts (and for your reference, Boo Boo's family rakes in $50,000 per show): '[Do] these stories and conversations of dieting, child pageants, pet pigs, food auctions, bad plumbing, bad breath contests, deer statues, toilet paper bombing, farting, belching, and sneezing cut too close to reality, and horrify? Or does this make us love them even more?'

I call up my friend April and tell her I can't write about Honey Boo Boo while the world is heaving. It is all part of this culture that I can't endure. She's a little black, April says, cutting to the chase.

This breaks me. I'm not hating on Boo Boo, am I?

There is a psychologist who writes about desire in Tehran. Maybe you have heard of her? Gohar Homayounpour. Her father is the Iranian translator of Kundera's *The Incredible Lightness of Being*. She writes about her perfect analysand. She writes about how this woman is both repulsed and in love with her own land. I could say I share this blessing. Is this also true for you? Isn't desire the ability to surpass the boundary, the brutal edge? a throwing of one's self? desire for what is wrong? desire of what is outlawed? desire that is about really seeing another, as Genet would have it, as one's self?

There is a photograph made years ago by Adam Bartos of a bare-chested, chubby boy in swim trunks balancing an outdoor grill grate on his head. Gazing at it, I realize that the power of the Boo Boo video is how Boo Boo has been made beautiful by someone who can see her; see her the way Bartos paints this half-naked chunk of a boy in the most honey-colored-end-of-afternoon light; see her the way Rembrandt saw *The Jewish Bride*. The bride 'has an ass,' Genet writes. 'You can tell.'

Jean Genet would have it that Rembrandt could only go one direction: in and through. He could only rid the subject of whatever anecdotal quality it had. He scrutinized and scrutinized until he no longer distorted anything with the effort of trying to make his paintings like anything or anyone. Yet he depersonalized nothing by oversimplification. 'Rembrandt presented what he painted,' Genet posits, 'as distinct substance—whether his subject was fields ploughed in the morning, smoking, or his own self daubing at a canvas, mad with color.' Genet, too, looked at photographs of criminals as though they were lovers, expecting, as Sontag notes, these representations to literally transform reality, or at least alter his own existence.

You tell me, Naveed, that this letter to you is untidy and advise me to let it sit, grow a patina. Instead, I take to it like a painter might, daubing and daubing until the surface is so thick it cracks. Look. Can you see in its glossy surface your own reflection? Soon, you will be touching down again on North American soil, coming for a visit to give a reading at the university where I teach. You say you are nervous for your upcoming week of whoring in New York, and then mention that a scarf screamed my name that you couldn't resist. You'll also come armed with my request (although I've asked you to pick up not the book but the author himself): Nadeem Aslam's *The Blind Man's Garden*. I'll stand the novel up on my shelf, the lemons on its cover unbearably yellow and plump. Genet, you know, veils the erotic by acting the saint, until, at the end of his essay on Rembrandt, he smashes his idol and admits he isn't really repulsed. Of course, he will love again. Of course!

A Short History of Torture

Dear George,

It is five in the morning and we are walking the wrong way through JFK International Airport. We do not know we are walking the wrong way; in fact, we have followed the signs. 'We' is perhaps a misnomer—for there has been no introduction. The signs now say something else. We are told, when we ask, that we must turn around. With a tired finger, a man in uniform points us back toward where we have just come.

We walk across what was once a 5,000-acre marsh inhabited by the Delaware, the Montaukett, and Shinnecock peoples. This is now the busiest U.S. gateway for those leaving by air. Every year more than 45 million people thread through this maze; forty billion dollars in wages and economic activity is distributed as a result, and the yearly value of transported cargo is double this amount.

In my knapsack is a book of letters sent between Jean Toomer and Waldo Frank. In your carry-on is at least one book by Manuel Zapata Olivella. Loaded with books, we turn and retrace our steps. Faced with a long corridor, I do not take the automated walkway. You remain in step beside me, assuming that we are coming from the same conference. We are. There is mention of this as we walk down the corridor in search of gate 24 for you and 25 for me. Everything else is history, a history so heavy it cannot be reduced to the books we carry.

But let us start here—with Olivella in your hands, for we are at my gate and I have asked you to repeat this author's name. So you reach into your bag and pull out the book. You are writing your dissertation on this man who traveled by foot from Colombia to New York in 1946. You speak now of Olivella's *Changó: The Biggest Badass*, a history of slave rebellion across the diaspora—Haiti, Brazil, Colombia, Venezuela, North America. You must know Changó? (You ask of the god, not the book.)

I nod. This thunderous spirit is a memory of feathers and scattered flower petals from the summer I worked in Brazil.

Already you are standing up, shaking my hand. It is time for you to catch your flight.

In the coming days, I will read *Changó: The Biggest Badass*, and, in Olivella's refusal to differentiate between past and present tenses, I will hear how rebellion continues. Holding the thick book that weighs so much that it physically hurts to read, I will judge myself no different from any of Olivella's white characters, who—no matter how noble or well-meaning—are never excused. ('As it should be,' you will email me.)

As it is, awaiting my delayed flight in the wake of your disappearance, I open *Brother Mine*, a collection of Toomer's and Frank's letters. What engages me is the literary hunger these men shared pre-Civil Rights and their commitment to social justice. Toomer's letters are those of a 27-year-old to a mentor—a literary father, so to speak. Frank's missives to Toomer are instructions, but also pleas to Toomer to help him 'write black.' Toomer plays the role of a doting literary son, happy enough to provide such expertise, but ultimately, as Changó would have it, he breaks free. He does so by sleeping with Frank's wife. Toomer writes in one of his last letters to Frank: 'Search and discovery bind us in the spirit, though no words break through the flesh.'

Reading this at the airport after your departure, I see again the scar that circles back behind your left ear, and wonder what you have made of my whiteness under airport lights. I watch a worker in uniform redirect the Starbucks line. Those in line block the flow of passenger traffic to the gates. My hand can still feel the flesh of your hand in this place that has perfected disappearances.

Here, on this once-upon-a-time marsh, genocide is still being waged. I can see, if I close my eyes, Maher Arar being apprehended while on a layover here. He is whisked away and held without charges for two weeks, questioned about his involvement with al-Qaeda, denied access to any lawyer, and then put on a small jet and flown to Jordan. There, he is blindfolded, shackled, and beaten. Then he is taken to a Syrian prison. That's where the real torture begins. He is made to falsely confess that he attended an al-Qaeda training camp as torturers beat his body with shredded cables. He is kept in a dark cell the length and width of his body for a year. Then, one day, seemingly out of the blue, Syrian officials confess that they can find nothing to link Arar to any plot. Canadian officials quickly apologize, fly him back to

Ottawa, and award him ten and a half million Canadian dollars to keep him, let's say, quiet.

A woman next to me is talking about how a former boyfriend met her at the airport with roses. I hate roses. They are so generic, she says. Get me something that says you know who I am.

I will learn, in the coming months, of how the U.S. murdered your father, who worked for Chiquita, by lining the pockets of Colombia's paramilitary. Before he was shot, your father had been a man who took his children to the ocean on his days off work, piling you all atop his bicycle and pedaling hard.

You and I will take to calling one another—you, a man whose father was killed by U.S.-backed assassins, and I, a woman trying to figure out what to do about her murderous country, and we will speak of loneliness, the limits of academic thinking, and, rather torturously, of love.

A Short History of Make Believe

Ophelia, airplane.

Grace is in her mother's arms, talking to my dog Ophelia. Up above is an airplane. Grace's brother Daniel throws a ball for Oph, and Oph lopes after it. Grace and Daniel's mother is a botanist, though she hasn't worked in four years. When Daniel was young she carried him, strapped to her, throughout the day, and every so often they would go deeper into the forest to nurse. Then he began walking, and she would pull a weed, and he would disappear. She's forgotten the names of the plants, she says. She had her flashcards out the other day.

We speak of losing connection to the earth. She says, I can't believe a day will go by, and I'll realize I haven't been outside.

Come evening, I tell a friend that I will read the new poems he's sent to me as soon as I am able to do so without crying too much. On the phone, I hear myself say that I read the first page of *Yellow Birds* and thought it brilliant, but that I didn't know whether I could read another book from that same point of view.

What do you mean? my friend asks. You mean from the soldier's—

Yes, I think so.

I know what you mean. I've been telling my counselors about the guilt that I have. About the children, the real children I watched suffer, he says. They are real. They are still there in Iraq. I'm here getting all this therapy and help, and they are over there. The therapists don't know what to say. They say, 'Don't think about that. You have to take care of yourself.'

Up above, there is no longer any airplane. The moon hangs like a little lump, a bobbin, a knitted cap. One hundred detainees are on hunger strike at Guantánamo. And a veteran of the war on terror is, at this moment, preparing to kill himself. He has spoken out about what it means to have been paralyzed fighting a war he thought was something else. In a filmed interview, he suddenly stops talking and bends over, feeling faint. His condition has something to do, he explains, with not being able to regulate his body temperature. His abdominal pain is so severe that he has had to seek treatment at a private medical facility that treats him, he says (speaking in short gasps and with a pronounced slur), much better than the VA hospital has. He has had his colon removed, but this hasn't eased his pain. He will end his life, he narrates stoically, with his wife by his side.

This afternoon, as Grace looked up at the airplane and Daniel threw balls for Oph, I imagined a child I brought over through the brambles playing in their backyard. But how, I think now, could I ever comfort a child from the world's horrors? Oph turns on her bed. For a moment, earlier, she had become a child among children, drinking Grace and Daniel's 'chicken noodle soup' out of their sled filled with water and dirt and sticks. Remember those days? Grace and Daniel's mother had asked me.

    I had nodded.

A Short History of Black Death

I never knew how much it cost to hunt rare animals, not to mention who could afford to shoot one. Of course, I was familiar with how close to extinction such animals were and had read of messy wars between conservationists, hunters, and poachers. I had read some Hemingway, too, but that, I thought, was just Hemingway. In any event, I never cared to talk to a big game hunter until one such hunter's sister hired me. During my interview, as I was being wined and dined, Cherise showed me her brother's picture in the bush with his kill.

Why? What subject had we broached? In the photo on Cherise's iPhone, her brother knelt, gun erect, behind *his* exotic animal. The restaurant was dark; the image glowed. The kill was a kudu, white horns spiraling upward. I now know that this is *the* typical safari photo, taken ritualistically after each slaughter, the head of the dead animal propped upon a mound of sand. He's one of the only African American safari hunters, Cherise said.

And it was this one fact—this hunter being an exception to some unwritten, age-old colonial rule coupled with the seeming incongruence of his actions (as if I thought any African American would understand the nature of oppression and carry that notion beyond his or her own person and so swear off the killing of all creatures) that awoke in me a curiosity. What was it that drove this particular man to travel to Africa to kill big game? Was his motivation—his, let's say, calling to kill, any different than a white man's? These were racist questions. This was, in fact, my own safari. I was just trading in the rifle for a pen.

As a white woman, I wanted this man's story to reveal some deeper relationship, some disturbance to a dangerous playing field I didn't understand. I wanted the bungled narrative to point to something I had not seen before, a larger truth, or at least to a complicated neocolonialist narrative about what it might mean for an African American to hire an African safari guide. You should write an essay about him, his sister suggested.

Flash forward: Herb drives his black Toyota pick-up truck up the driveway to the goat farm where I live. I watch from my window in the barn loft. I'm trying to hurry. He gets out and stands under the Kentucky coffee tree. I half-run down the sloping green hill, shouting, Hi, I'm Spring.

Before I hop into the passenger seat of this hunter's vehicle, before he drives me north, following the automated female voice on his GPS, know this: I milk goats, shovel their shit, and attempt to care for their well-being. However, I am also fully aware that pastoralism marks the beginning of unrestrained consumerist mentalities, and that hunting—at least before animals were grown like plants, selectively bred, stocked in game preserves and boxed in factories—was once dependent upon the savvy of selectivity and restraint. If one overhunted or polluted one's hunting ground that was the end of one's food source. In many respects, before the human population skyrocketed, hunters' lives were more sustainable and their nomadic lifestyles better for the planet. The farmer-induced capitalist mentality, in other words, is perhaps the mentality that has done more to exterminate the brute, should we say, than any other mentality in history.

I guide Herb down Yellow Springs Road to Route 113, assuring him, as we round another bend that we haven't gone too far. On the phone in March, I had explained my motivation to write this essay. I had framed it as hinging upon my own interest in animals, purposefully dancing around the subject of race, as white people often do. I had told him that I lived and worked on a farm and was interested in the differences between hunter and herder. That's cool that you work with goats and can swing with my sister, Herb had commented.

Your sister tells me that you're one of the only African American safari hunters, I say now, switching the subject away from the explanation of why I didn't attend the end-of-semester faculty party.

I think right now I'm the only one, or one of the only ones, Herb says, turning us onto Route 113. There was one my PH—professional hunter—told me about who hunted a while ago. But that's not why I hunt: to be one of the few. I hunt for the thrill of it.

Like a matador? I ask. It just pops out.

Yes.

I'm surprised. Matadors, in my imagination, are magicians with capes, pulling long-horned bulls out of pockets. Choosing to brush with death seems like a cultural ritual and more dangerous than hunting game with a rifle from a ridge. Bullfights, in my mind, are fairer to the animal (even given the long *banderillas* driven into bulls' backs and the years of study matadors put in before stepping out into the ring). Hunters' guns, bullets, and the long distances they maintain from their game make killing a bull by hand seem particularly unfair.

They call Africa the motherland, Herb is saying. When I came back after my first safari, after seeing how people over there live, how rough they have it, he continues, I thought I should call myself just American—not African American.

I'm intrigued. The comment reminds me of journalist Keith B. Richburg's account of being African American in Africa and feeling unhinged by the experience. It reminds me, too, of a poem I once read. I ask Herb whether he has read Toi Derricotte.

No, who's that?

She's a poet, and in one of her books, she describes going to Africa and an African telling her that she was lucky her family had been enslaved. (It is telling that I do not speak of repatriating African Americans, of Liberia, Garvey.)

What?

I guess the point was that Toi's life as a black living in America today was better—

Oh, I see what you're saying. You're making me really think here.

Who am I to quote Toi Derricotte? I steal a look at Herb. His profile is flat; he wears wire-rimmed glasses. He doesn't seem like a hunter; he seems quiet, introspective, unassuming—or, as he describes himself, reserved.

You know, I went back and reread *Green Hills of Africa*, I say.

You did?

(Herb had mentioned this book on the phone.) Yes, I guess it made me think, mostly, of the manly aspect of big game hunting.

Huh, I've never thought about it that way before.

Really?

I guess it *is* mostly a man's sport.

Are there women safari hunters? I ask.

I don't know. I don't think there are many. I mean they might go with their husbands.

We're heading north to Douglasville to meet Aaron, his taxidermist. A few months ago, Cherise had told me that Herb had been leafing through some magazine and had seen photographs of his trophies. Those are my animals, he'd told Cherise. I should get a cut.

The taxidermist had won some award for best-preserved or something, Cherise had said. Herb didn't get a cut. But he was right—they were his animals.

The night she'd told me this, I had Googled the taxidermist and found a thank you note from Herb on Aaron's website: 'Your attention to detail is impeccable and very much appreciated. Thanks for bringing my trophies back to life.' Aaron, too, was quoted in an article linked to the site saying that 'people think of taxidermy as almost a redneck industry.' He, however, had insisted that what he did was 'an art.'

It's raining when Herb and I pull up to Aaron's. We've traveled an hour. It's now 1:01 p.m., according to the clock on Herb's truck's dash. I said we'd be here at one. Look at that, Herb says.

I knew you'd be here exactly at one, Aaron says, standing in the mouth of his open garage.

Aaron is tall and has an easy grin. His cheeks look like he's hiding golf balls in them. The garage looks like any other garage from the outside. But inside, one wall is lined with mounted deer, ibex, springbok, blesbok, and zebra heads. Pins stick out of the animals' noses, eyes, foreheads. Plastic forms shaped like skulls litter a workbench.

Do you have any water? Herb asks. We've done so much talking on the drive here, I'm hoarse.

Don't have water, but you guys want Zeroes? It's what I drink. Gotta watch my girlish figure. Aaron laughs and hands me a can of Diet Coke.

I crack open the tab as he shows us tubs of colored epoxy that he uses to patch furless spots on cracking mounts. The soda pop swims in my mouth. Let's go to the studio, Aaron suggests.

Before we go, Herb needs to use the restroom. He asks for an umbrella as it has begun to rain. There is none. I watch him half-run across the drive to Aaron's house from the foyer of a house that's been transformed into a showroom for Aaron's specimens. He still doesn't seem like a hunter, I catch myself thinking.

In the studio, I cringe before a stuffed giraffe head and neck, an entire Alaskan Brown Bear, a lion reclining on the rug, and the poachers' spears that Aaron says he brought back from Mozambique. (When his father refinished them, Aaron tells me that he cursed him out: Why'd you do that? They were authentic!)

When Herb returns, he points to a pedestal. I want that for my Cape Buffalo. How much is that?

Which one? The one with the Africa cutout?

Yeah. I like that. Hey, I want to ask you: Do you think going on safari is manly?

I've been reading Hemingway? Have you read him? I ask Aaron, butting in.

Hell ya, it's manly. Nah, I haven't read Hemingway. Want to, though.

I look at Herb. As a child, he wanted to run away to the Rocky Mountains. Instead, he fell in love with his teacher Mrs. Edmunds—a woman who helped him with his special learning needs. He wanted to go back to visit her after he finished graduate school to show her his diploma and thank her, but she had just passed. As a teen, he'd gotten excited about big game hunting while working at a sporting goods store, making eight dollars an hour and helping service people who were going on safari. He knew he would never be able to afford to go on such a hunt himself if he continued to work for eight bucks an hour, and this was what had inspired him, he'd told me on the drive to Aaron's, to go to college.

Aaron shuttles us up the white-carpeted stairs to the studio attic where his computer is on and begins to click through his photos. Of course, I am interested in the images on the screen. I am sickened by the stuffed animals below me, but the hunt—the process that opens these men up to the wilderness and connects them with other forms of life—captivates me. I want to know more about what drives Herb and Aaron to walk crotch-deep into leech-infested waters, crawl on their bellies across savannahs, and turn themselves into killing machines.

I watch as, in one video Aaron plays for us, a hulk of a cat falls from a tree. I hear Aaron comment about how mean she was.

It is wrong, I think. Wrong to do this.

Herb sees it differently. They are culling the herd, memorializing an animal no one would otherwise ever remember. They are keeping game alive, preserving populations of wild beasts against poachers who plunder without paying to replenish.

Later, in a diner over a grilled cheese, I confess to Herb that I have been trying to adopt a child from Africa.

That's cool, Herb says. Maybe you'll inspire my sister!

I don't reveal that the adoption will cost roughly the same amount that Herb pays for a safari. I can still hear the crack of the gun and the thud of the cat hitting the ground. We finish our fries and Herb drives me back to the goat farm.

A Short History of Genetics

Osama bin Laden's body was supposedly cast into the sea.

~

The sperm arrived in a cardboard box with a smiley face drawn around the punched out handle. The woman at the FedEx station scanned its barcode into a computer. I stood on the other side of the counter beside the bubble wrap, packing tape, and unfolded boxes. The box was three feet tall, rectangular, and on its side was a sticker publishing the fact that it contained human tissue. It was a hot day—at least 90 degrees. I felt revolted by the box, by having to haul its incredibly visible size around. I sat it next to me on my truck's bench seat and drove out of the lot.

~

The official story goes like this: before bin Laden's murder, Pakistani doctor Shakil Afridi, wooed by the CIA, was ordered to set up a vaccination drive for Hepatitis B, so as to gain access to bin Laden's compound.

     Seymour Hersh retells this story. According to Hersh, Amir Aziz, a doctor and major in the Pakistani army, was the real CIA informant who moved next door to the very ill bin Laden, oversaw his medical treatment, and, after procuring the DNA sample that confirmed bin Laden was actually bin Laden, received a cut of the $25 million that the U.S. paid to a number of Pakistani informants.

     Stories aside: if bin Laden's DNA was really drawn, who is now doing what with its spiraling double helix?

~

After testing my urine, convinced I missed the window of opportunity, I called the midwife and said something about it being an expensive error. She argued, You've got it; might as well put it in there.

I drove to Springwood Road, my hair uncombed, glasses sliding down my nose. We'll need gloves, I said, as soon as I'd hauled the box inside the midwife's office.

I have them, she assured me.

Not rubber gloves. I mean mittens or something, I said. I just read the instructions.

Oh, you mean it's like dry ice in there?

She retrieved a fireplace mitt. She looked like a welder, even in her thin-strapped gown, as she put on the mammoth glove and opened the tank. Inside the smoking bomb-like case was a vial the size of a pea. It's so small, she exclaimed.

I laughed.

~

As reported in no objective terms in the now contested *New Yorker* article, the Navy SEAL Six Team descended from the air on ropes, but the first helicopter, disguised, so as not to be seen or heard, got caught in its own rotor wash. It was a moonless night. The SEAL team swarmed. Some men blew up the compound's door hinges. Thirty-eight minutes later, the SEAL team's mission complete, a medic drew blood, two bone marrow samples, and swabbed the dead bin Laden. A genetic kinship analysis was thereafter performed. The test claimed, with 99.9 percent certainty, that the body was really his.

~

I wanted to read Langston Hughes—the sperm donor's favorite author—as I lay on the bed, letting the thawed sperm swim, but I had forgotten the book. Instead, I opened up *The Prosthetic Impulse* (complete with a womanish cyborg with shirt pulled up to reveal an apple-red, plastic-looking child in utero on its cover) and read about the inductive process of cloning sheep. Natural reproductive processes, during which sperm and egg fuse into one, are, the text read, deductive. A sentence: 'Sex, in short, is anti-replication,' reminded me of what a man had once said when I had informed him that my father's cancer diagnosis had triggered in me a horrible yearning for a child. Cancer, he had said, is endless replication.

~

A dog named Cairo reportedly joined the 79-person team that raided bin Laden's compound. *The New York Times* ran a photo series that same week on dogs that deploy. I clicked on images of dogs in fields, walking through Iraqi streets, jumping from helicopters, and wasn't surprised by the lack of inclusion of photographs of dogs snarling in foreign prisons with pools of blood on the floor and persons in orange clothing cowering.

~

The CIA's fake vaccine drive, regardless which doctor—Afridi or Aziz—oversaw it, wreaked havoc on the Pakistani prime minister's special polio vaccination program (setting back an already fragile effort to vaccinate a polio-infected nation) by feeding into the fear of those Pakistanis who believe that vaccinations are part of a Western sterilization campaign against Muslims. Can anyone blame them? (And can anyone tell me why Afridi is being tortured in Pakistani prison?)

~

After the procedure, I pulled on my clothes, and drove home. I felt uneasy—not unlike how I had felt when my friend Amos took me for a ride in his new black bug and his mother's voice emerged from the car's surround-sound speakers. I remember sitting there, in the middle of (as if *inside* their phone conversation) and feeling like I was back in the theater watching *Pinocchio* as a child—a film I had to be carried out of, so devastated was I by the idea of being swallowed by a whale.

~

We got him, President Obama said on that May 1st night.

Who did we get? Who was bin Laden aside from a man murdered (in total disregard of international law) in front of one of his wives and his 12-year-old daughter?

~

There is a short story by Asli Erdogan about a pregnant woman who finds herself hoping that her baby will have a better life than she does, even though she doesn't think the baby will. She sits in a café and the waiter forgets her tea. When he finally brings it, she doesn't want it anymore.

~

This is the era of genetics—at least Siddartha Mukherjee, author of the definitive biography of cancer, says so. Whatever era it is, this is not a world in which one should get pregnant by mail.

~

This is what happened: I sent the box back, its smiley face still smiling.

A Short History of Labor

> Or it is the wrung breast of one
> human family's need and of an
> owner's taking, yielding blood and
> serum in its thin blue milk...
> —James Agee

Barn and Surrounds

I live in the barn. In return for work on the farm, I receive a discount in rent. Life isn't pastoral; it's physical, animal. Bats fly in and flies. The rafters are high and a ladder remains from when the living room filled with hay. Neighbors mow their lawns like crazy, the hood suburban, a farm development for the rich—horse farms, mostly. Up the way, mansion windows look out at nuclear power plant towers.

Assembly

Waiting to be milked, goats huddle under the black walnut in the rain. Inside the milk room, I wedge the green feed containers specked with grain and goat spit between metal headpieces on the milk stand. Each goat gets a scoop of grain topped with pink calf manna. From the rack above the sink, I lift down buckets and set them atop dollies. The buckets' empty silver mouths gape. I press black gaskets into the bucket lids to cushion the pulsators. They're fragile. If they fall apart, I have to snap them back. If the knurl nuts won't untwist, the pulsators are on wrong. I force milk lines and silicone inflations onto lid ends, and hook up the main lines. Unoiled dolly wheels scream as I push the decorated buckets to the opposite end of the milk room. There I feed the black hoses to the vacuum valves and snake the other ends to the lids. The floor is now brown from what's been tracked in. Soon, the goats will track in more and I'll have to clean everything.

Muck in Greece

The raking of hillsides has become my pastime. A few years ago, I collected horse shit on Corfu, shoveling it into grain sacks, and setting ammonia-laden stacks of straw on fire. Goat shit weighs less. I pitch it and the wet straw into a wheelbarrow and push it all uphill to the trailer. Sometimes a teetering happens at the trailer's lip. Once or twice I've had to ease the barrow down the corrugated metal ramp backward when it's wet and my tennis shoes don't grip. It was raining hard on Crete when I was as a child and a family of boys took me out to the barn. The glee we had in the wet muck!

I put my hood up and wheel the empty barrow back behind the hay barn.

Farmers' Market

The garden crew arrive on skateboards with afro Mohawks, high-tops and doggy backpacks. They take green gourds out of buckets and set to work tying up bunches of basil. I set out samples of cheese next to the cupcake man. One of the girls who sell fresh-roasted coffee compliments the man on his fat white watch. She asks which cupcake he recommends. A mother shopping with her different daughter says she's curious about my different life. She recently left her city cubicle to be a stay-at-home mom. Some of the cheese is smooth. One kind, Purple Passion, tastes like lavender. I say it's my favorite. Maybe you're my kind of woman, a balding man tries. He tells me he can't eat cheese—No more quadruple bypasses, and then says something about a woman he knew who worked out to look good in a coffin.

I clasp my hand over my mouth. That's awful, I say. I don't tell him I once thought this way. I didn't eat.

I smell basil as the kids continue to twist twistums around their green bouquets. There's no better scent. Clouds gather above watermelons. A woman brings me two peaches. Grill them, and put your goat cheese on top, she says.

I sit on an empty milk crate. Across from me, the two coffee roasting girls with silver bullet thermoses share a cloth chair, their bare, lithe legs as carefully thinned as the bunches of basil. One of the gardeners tries to engage them. They're cordial and even laugh when he dips his doggy backpack down into their dog dish.

Moon Reflected

I thought today of how all I wanted was a goat bell for my tenth birthday, and remembered Manos making milk rounds in his truck and the *yayas* coming out with whatever they had milked, the golden rounds of hard cheese floating in brine in Manos's brother's basement. My father photographed the yellow rinds in low light and was astonished later to discover how still he'd stood.

Production

Shut gate. Lead goats in, five at a time. Make sure vacuum works. Lock heads in. Wipe udders, teats first. Strip milk, two squirts. Hook up pumps. Milk. Flip off vac. Spray teats with Antibac. Unlock goats and lead out. Shut door. Reload food. Next five goats in. Lock. Wash hands. Repeat until last goat out. Turn off vac. Pick up all used wipes and discard. Shut off left vac. Change over suction system to sink. Depress inflation tabs. Rinse. Place in middle basin and let soak. Unhook black vac hoses and hang above door. Weigh milk. Each bucket weighs nine pounds. Subtract. Place paper sieve in huge funnel. Take off shoes. Pour milk through sieve into holding tank. Keep lights off. Clean milk buckets. Inflations go in third sink. Sweep floor. Clean sieve. Hang up inflations, tabs up. Stack milk buckets face down to dry with sieve. Clean vac tubes. Wash floor. Hang inflations up to dry. Wash black hoses. Drain sinks. Take off boots. Shut off light.

A Short History of Overproduction

Surplus of food due to mechanization, insecticides, fertilizers. Food prices plummet, farmers let crops rot, kill animals. Government programs raise food prices and pay landowners subsidies to grow soil-enriching crops and for land left idle. Soviet purchase of North American grain increases exports. Farm incomes and food prices skyrocket. Farmers buy land and machines. High interest rates and record harvests lead again to overproduction. Food prices fall. Foreclosed land is sold off. Huge agribusinesses buy it up. Agribusinesses force farmers to sow genetically manufactured seed. Small farmers can't compete. In India, unable to feed their families, farmers commit suicide en masse. In North America, farmers struggle to find reliable workers and hire immigrants. Police raid farms. Ship workers back. Artificial insemination breeds super-producing livestock. Overpro-duction ensues and with it a surplus of food.

Territorial Challenges
In Pakistan, two men make breakfast slowly; the heat marries them to their thin clothes. Their lips dance around lemon rinds in Lipton teas. In Penn-sylvania, goats are locked into headpieces, teats hooked to vacuums. The dog stops barking, but last night's dream still haunts my peripheral vision. Goats' pupils are horizontally oblong to better see peripherally. I tell the dog that tomorrow she will undergo an operation to remove her ovaries. Today is the day we blew up the world in 1945. Now our robotic weap-ons fly around the two men in Lahore. When the day breaks with dew, when there are innumerable sufferings, what does one do? Feed straw to the goats. The story goes: one goat wouldn't, then came into heat on a night right in time for an ice storm. A trailer driven on the icy roads to find a male goat? The neighbor goat would have to do. The resulting kids have tiny ears. The first casualty of war is truth. Can you hear a drone? I am not sure about what it means to breed or kill. I know more about the economy of unisexual lizard life. I never was a people person, but increasingly I've become a peopleless person.

Queens of the soon-to-be baking city of Lahore look out: the U.S. military has modified goats, injecting them with spiders' genes. At first, we tried to harvest webs directly, but the spiders revolted, grew violent, killed one another. Injected goats give webbed milk without fuss. When woven into armor, goat silk is strong—almost bulletproof. I'll send you some to put it on, so you can drink tea without worry out on your balcony.

End of the Line
I drop my dog off to be spayed. Humans do anything we want to animals. The next day a father and his two sons come to pick up their mutt. I join them in line, seven a.m., kids dressed to the nines, father giving out fist bumps. There's a man behind us who's just so happy, he says, to have his cat spayed.

Traffic peals as my dog wakes from her fog, belly scarred. I give her a stuffed squirrel, feeling guilty. And she prances.

Let Us Now Praise Eduardo
The first time I saw him, he was dressed in a straw hat and button-up plaid shirt. His stomach was flat. He looked my age, perhaps a few years older. This made me happy. The hat and shirt made his work with the goats look bearable. He didn't seem overheated, in other words. His skin the color of tanned leather. If I romanticize this migrant, it is because I don't understand what it is like to be dismissed, disappeared, for there to be no record. Please do not excuse this oversight; make use of it, memorize Eduardo leading the goats to be milked in this heat up this ever so gently sloping hillside.

I Call Them All Mom
Those I knee out the door (who know how to wiggle the latch and let themselves in and whose feet hurt so badly they walk on their knees) have been pregnant countless times, each kid stolen from them at birth. What gives them the stamina to go on? How can Renata look so content as she hobbles over after being milked to take a sip from the big green bucket of spring water? I've lost the spring to my step. I pour the goats' milk into the stainless steel holding tank.

Naveed
I remember goats near the turn off for the university in your Lahore, there where the barber shaves men and kids play billiards outdoors. You, the poet, on the roof of the school, took me under your wing, showed me *La Passion de Jeanne D'Arc*. I had seen it before with another gay man, someone I loved who turned cruel. Goats, I've read, come into heat as regularly as humans do. They flag their tails near bucks, grow vocal, and supposedly lose their appetites.

After I left Pakistan, I knew I was alone. I began testing my LH surge—in goats it is called the male effect, as it depends upon exposure to bucks' sordid stink. If the buck is not separated from the doe, his scent will permeate her milk. I could measure my fertility, but without the curry soaking through my skin from those colorful spices patted into pyramids in the venders' alleys of Lahore, what could I do? You found a lover who needed regular blood transfusions. When I wrote to you of my sadness, you heard a crimson melancholy in my tone. After birthing, when goats hear the pump go on, have their udders wiped, and taste the grain, their pituitary glands expand and their milk lets down. Did you know, Naveed, goat milk is naturally homogenized? The cream remains, instead of rising, suspended—

One Lost Goat
This morning, Pixie (a rubber tie around what was once a cyst in her jaw) bawled. I let her out of the stall and she followed, screaming whenever she couldn't see me.

Mama Heart
I used to go to Mama Heart's for daycare. She knit me a long pink sweater I grew into over the years. I think of her—not what she looked like, but the sound of her name, when Heart, the eldest of the herd, lies down in the field of red grasses, arthritis making it too hard for her to stand.

Centaur
The buck ran down the hill. I held the rope circling his neck with my left hand and grabbed at old fence posts with my right. Slivers dug into my fingers. I laughed. Inside the fenced field, I let him go—beard wild, scrotum low. Later, waiting for an elevator, I tried to curl my upper lip like him. I had to grin and squint to get it up.

Fieldwork
She was in the grass, a brown and black snowflake, hair up, droplets of dew on her back. I didn't touch or remove her from the path. I wanted her to know that there was room. History corrodes and the future doesn't look bright. She can survive, I've read, an Arctic winter. First her heart stops beating, then her gut freezes, and lastly her blood. In the spring, she thaws and pupates. When it's all said and done, she flies around with only days to mate before the end. The least I could do was leave her woolly body as I happened upon it.

Surfing

Who would I be had my parents promised me, way back when, to one of those Greek boys who raced my father's bicycle in the rain and taught me how to surf on goat shit? When I'm milking, or pitching hay, I don't think about adopting a child from another country or three children from Nebraska. I don't get online and surf the net for those who wait with malformed heads. If I think of whether I can afford to parent a seven-year-old who is HIV positive, I don't replay the worry ad nausea. Instead, the wheelbarrow needs to be emptied and I'm always mad, because there's a concrete step to roll up or down, and the shit is heavy.

Because Adoption Is So Questionable

Do you know the face of your child before you conceive? Is it ingrained? Between the steering wheel and signal switch: a spider web. I leave it, fearing that when I change direction it might break. The man was not trying to teach me, even though he thought he was, when he kicked me and said, Make a fucking decision, and make it a good one.

When you milk a goat, stroke her. Imagine giving your milk away. I've entered middle age with trepidation and back pain. Life doesn't make much sense, I tell Sean, whose girlfriend had a heart attack and passed.

Sean is in college. Like him, I don't know how to desire any longer. It all backs up into past sadness, as if plumbing gunk got in there and my father couldn't lift the snake to fish it out. When we did this together, my pop and I, soap grease had virtually closed the pipe; inside was a white mass that stank as badly as my dog does now. When the skunk's musk hit her this morning, I saw her go down, muzzle in the grass, trying to wipe the sting from her eyes. I remember getting mad at my father telling me what to do, how to operate the snake, and the stench making my head hurt down in the basement. I decide suddenly that I will check on a child. I will send a check to the crooked agency operating without check in a poor, poor land to find out whether the girl with HIV isn't still available, and by this I mean alive, because once upon a time (how can a year feel so long?) her laughing face and sideways cornrows made imagining a daughter possible.

American Gothic

My folks built their first home for what I pay for one month's rent, so when the farm owner who makes cheese three days a week and his wife (who tells others where to plant trees) ask me to work an extra day because one of their staff is out sick, I say no.

Look at this photo. My mom's head is covered in a dishrag. My father holds up a broom like it's a pitchfork. They stand in front of an old army tent (in which they lived while building that first one-thousand dollar home), a stovepipe threading right through its canvas.

Clover Tea

I wanted my own farm, searched for a parcel of scrub on which to build a shack. Tiny houses were the rage, but I didn't have money enough to make anything work. So I settled on someone else's dream, moved in, and began to work. I woke the first morning with a tick on my shoulder. Soon it was ninety-one degrees and the sores on my body from lifting and sweating began to ooze. I'll get pregnant, I told myself, on the night of the full moon. So I ordered a tomcat catheter from a pet supply store, calculated when the right days of the month were, contacted a midwife who lived down the road, and decided the child would grow to be large. Such a being wasn't to be. In my new home, complete with goats below me, I should have known not to drink so much clover tea. I should have watched the goats nuzzle up against the fence where the bucks humped and pranced. Instead, I thought I could go it alone, do everything myself.

The Price of Cheese

Staff are paid less to milk mechanically then they would make if they milked by hand (because milking by hand takes longer). There is heavy lifting of grain sacks involved. One continually bends over the goats to wipe udders, strip teats, and monitor inflations. No special training is required. A migrant worked here, but was recently let go, as he did not—the farm owner informed me—understand the productivity of this operation.

Eduardo did not complete his tasks within the time frame allocated and was spotted wiling away clocked hours. The price of cheese is high, but so is the cost of alfalfa. Neighbors complain about the smell. I have never smelled anything untoward and I live in the barn.

Now I know how black families must have felt, the farm owner informs me, standing beside the in-ground swimming pool in back of the barn on his million-dollar farm.

Hungry Virgins
On Sundays, I feed the kids at Hollow Road. They scream as soon as they catch wind of me. I try to halve the bale of hay before I reach the field, but they're already all over me. They scream again because I haven't brought their grain. Pouring grain into the trough around their hungry heads is like threading a needle blind. Then there's screaming again when I cross the field along the dirt worn path to fill their water. They run in bulk. Locked in the courtyard are the teens; they scream loudest. If I didn't know they were goats, I would think I was hearing humans being tortured. I wheel the barrow through the barn, unlatch the door, and rake up pissed-on straw. A garden hose hangs on a stripped paint roller. I shake it down and fill up the inside metal basin. On my way out, again they holler.

Skunked
At quarter to five, I walk my dog down Street Road. We swim through humid air and thick clouds of pollen. We're up early. Otherwise, there's too much traffic. Big Oph runs loose. Headlights swing. I call her close. A car passes, leaving perfume in its wake. The stink gives me an instant headache.

Remains of the Day's Events
My hands reek of saline and sweat. Beneath my bedroom, the milk room's wet. Earlier, I hung the milk pail on the door after feeding the bucks in the dark—too long an evening, shadowed by a younger girl. Everyone who worked here back when I arrived has left or been let go; now there are young white faces, eager until the end of the day when, harried, they change clothes, climb into cars, and zip away. Today Heart and Topaz didn't want to be milked; they kicked and fussed. I felt slightly nonplussed being watched by this newbie. On the radio I learned of children dead of lead poisoning leaked from Nigerian mines. Lately, I've been drawn again to photographs of waiting children adoption agencies cull and pawn. The kids whose images I study similarly face the direst deaths—like the one whose

photo I studied for months and months. At first I was told she was healthy. Last year, too, they said her father was alive. Now she has an older sister. The girl herself has grown up overnight. She's no longer toothless. What happens to harden us? Today the goats were led all day, one by one, into a stall to be mated with one of two bearded bucks. This evening the girl with whom I milked said she saw the remains of the day's events on the goats' hind ends. I didn't look. I didn't want to acknowledge all that life entails. Instead, I tried to calm Heart, my head pressed into her side, milk leaving her body as she stamped out her protest.

Three Women

Caroline has Lyme disease. She rides the tractor across the lawn. It hurts to walk. She feels old; her joints ache. She's quitting the farm to work at the health food store where there are benefits and no ticks.

Sheryl picks up the young buck. He doesn't struggle. It's pouring. She's in raingear. A lot of breeding went on today, she says. I wanted to change the hay. I hope they're enjoying themselves anyway.

Maria wears scrubs to milk. She brings her radio and plays the goats hard rock. She leaves detailed messages on the white board and always follows what she writes with: 'Clean up all milk!'

Two Lost Goats

Twins are better than one, as twins are usually smaller. The stillborn was big and the mother's pelvis tiny.

Upward Mobility

The turkey vultures were waiting in the trees for us. Or so it seemed. My dog and I spooked them from some forest feast. At least thirteen flew slant, then over us, bodies seemingly too heavy to lift. I felt cursed, walking beneath them in the valley with its bad air and insane traffic. Death lurked. At least they could lift up.

The Neighbors

An older couple live near the dairy where migrant workers congregate on dark mornings, their packs stashed under the farmhouse eaves. The couple is kind and the man, like my father, off-balance with age. The woman's asymmetrical face shows signs of a stroke. I was walking by when they exclaimed over my dog: She's a horse; she'd bowl me over.

I kept tight hold of Oph's collar. You going around on Elbow Road? the man wanted to know.

I said I was.

They nodded, That's a pretty way.

They were sanity surrounded by Republican Party signs on lawns of unaffordable property after unaffordable property in this 25th wealthiest county in the United States.

Truth and Lies

Yesterday, the farm owner told me someone was after their goats. A suspicious group of men, he said, in a white windowless van have been hanging out on Hollow Road.

I thought the news a little odd. Who would steal a goat?

The farm owner's wife surmised Eduardo was talking. Hispanic people, she went on, eat goat. There are a lot of immigrants around and he is friendly with that community.

My father devoted his life to eradicating racism. He took part in the Civil Rights Movement. When he and my mom began to farm, they did what they had been advocating black farmers do and became self-sufficient.

Recently, my dad who is crippled with cancer and can barely walk taught me how to use a chainsaw. The first thing I sawed was a downed tree with a trunk not much bigger than my leg. Next I felled a thirty-foot standing dead birch. I cut the notched mouth, then backed around and tried to match the cut. I was too low. So I cut again, higher. Stopped. Deeper. Finally, the tree began to lean. Then it let go.

October Evening

There is no one, nothing, just the omnipresent pumps sucking in the milk room. I am cold. The barn not yet heated. How can I ever mother alone? I cannot imagine. I cannot imagine never being a mother more. Tears, as I try to understand why I'm here. My nose is chapped, just like Heart's teats are. The utter fear, not knowing how to locate myself after so many dislocations—town after town. I want to take a hot bath, but can't find the stopper.

24-Hour Surveillance
If you ask me, it's overkill—laminated signs of video cameras on the barn and each pen post. It works on me, though. Big brother watches as I fork wet straw into the barrow, and as I swear after knocking over the bucket of water I've filled for the bucks who try to get with the girls as soon as I open the gate. I don't think: Well, fire me then! Although I can't really be fired, the farm owners could request I relocate. I used to be brazen. Now I feel like every goat is me. After milking, I look them in the eyes. It's a little gesture, something other than a mechanical eye trained to apprehend a subject.

Heart's Last Season
I lean into Heart's rib cage and press her hip up against the agricultural mesh to try to calm her. It hurts to give milk. It hurts, too, to tell one's life story to a stranger who thinks your parents are crazy, believes in some other political purpose, and calls your home interesting. She does not shake my hand when she leaves—this arbiter who will present my childless case and intent to adopt to the State. She says some people think too much of their genetic makeup. I rage on about eugenics. She and I share certain opinions when it comes to race. But I sob after she's gone because I feel I've prostituted myself. What is this game of wanting a child? What is this need for milk? Heart, tell me: Is there a better way? How should I approach when you are on your knees? You are tired, are you not? If it were up to me, I would let you dry up immediately.

Capitalism
Hunter-gatherers could never overeat; their food supply would have vanished. Pastoralism thusly marked the beginning of consumerism and mass production. As I watch Topaz and Heart on their knees, hooves tender, I lose all appetite for cheese. One might say I overreact, the goats' lives are luxurious; don't they have a nice stall overflowing with fresh straw? Don't they eat no-spray hay and specially formulated grain and hang out all day on a beautiful hillside? To which I might respond: how do they feel? With goats five to the stand, milking tubes hooked up to vacuums, I bend over the industrial sink and scrub the stainless steel buckets.

Meat and Cheese

The sun has passed over the tent. In several jackets, I sell cheese to those carrying pumpkins. Someone leaves potatoes by the table leg. Beside me, the wine woman sells her sparkling and tells of buying land after her husband got laid off and of their trips to Germany to get grapes to age right. Ahead is the man who always smiles. He does a business with twelve coolers and his teenage daughters. The man sells meat, eggs, and potpies, and seems too kind to kill and butcher. Two small black girls show up at his tent. Perched atop the meat man's coolers with the sun back-lighting them, the girls share an apple with one of the meat man's daughters. Then a woman arrives with a long lens on her camera. She looks like the older girls, and is white like the meat man, but even the younger girls call this woman mom.

You've got a great family, I tell the man.

A lot of energy, he says and smiles.

Spring Fed

Slip of water over stone, milk bucket on a nail. In the farm owner's dining room: a Wyeth print of a table with a cup on it.

Belonging

This is where she lives. My mother's drawn the barn in a diary I gave her. She shows the drawing to a friend.

I remember the day my mother made this sketch. It was the same day she and my father lay in my bed and listened to the goat bells and spoke of how appropriate it was—my living here. I love it when my parents speak in bed. It is almost too beautiful. All the prickly arguments are put away, and they enjoy what they say and having someone to say it to.

Milk Room

Rejoice is always first in line. Rena wears a bell. Peek-a-boo has the runs. Secret jitters on the stand, squeezes her legs and squats until the inflations pop off. Topaz knocks her feed bucket off its ledge. Hoofs bang the door. The pump hums. I move around in gumboots several sizes too large and whisper to Secret. I milk 38 pounds, a record for this late in the season. I'm in a good mood. Everything's easy today, even the difficult goats.

134

A Trick
Under the full moon, toilet-papered trees glow. The day after blood was sent to Idaho for Peek's pregnancy test, she was flirting with Mo over the fence. Anyone knows now she's not with kid. My fingers are cracking, my elbows have grown tight, and my belly's full of curry. I want to show. I want everyone to know I'm adopting a child—just as tonight, on this road, moonlight adopts whatever it touches.

Settled
You call a goat settled after the buck's rut no longer makes her wild. Pregnant, all of them, and still giving. My adoption application has been approved. I must make room. There is such thing as rhythm. There is such thing as blessing the moon for its light on a night after milking when the goats are tired, hungry, and streaming through the gate—all except for Heart who stops and nudges me to rub her nubby head. I urge her on. Time to open the gates; time to bed down.

Frozen
Cuddy calls, still lost after losing her two. A swollen time, this end of February. Earlier, I sat on straw and felt almost kid, stripping her milk. Sheryl shows me photos of the dead kids on her phone. Cuddy cleaned them and everything, she says.

I don't want to see, but I look. How exquisitely formed and beautiful they are, not all white and stiff like I'd pictured.

Misgivings
The baby buck is struggling. The third kid took too long and died inside Rejoice. What is this kidding business? As I muck, my rake uncovers a placenta, buried in straw—proof of how bloody labor is.

Invisible Hands
The assembly line's become a concrete floor of illusory profit. Milk is suctioned and bubbles. Online, the farm looks like a fairy-tale. On the ground, workers toil. Outsourcing: who do you think makes the goat caramel, the cheesecakes, cuts the shrubs, cleans the house? The farm owners are,

self-proclaimed, still in the red. I hang up the milk lines, hose down the dirty floor, and turn off their lights.

Two Mothers

The stall is split: Heart on one side, D.D. on the other—each with their triplets. Heart's a good mother; her kids are up and jumping. D.D. has a history of killing her kids. I try to get them to take her teats. She won't have it, paws the straw down to the sawdust. Her kids shiver.

Deliver Me

When I saw the hooves, I ran to tell the farm owner's wife. She came with towels and plastic gloves, and reached up into Hope and pulled out Honor. It took two tries, then a buck followed. Justice was covered in thick goo. We warmed the kids and toweled them off as they sneezed and nickered. Hearing them, D.D. wandered over. She licked Honor's head. Go away, D.D., the owner's wife shouted.

I held onto Honor, wishing never to have wanted to become a mother.

When Magic Died, she was birthing. One kid survived. Two were born dead. The farm owner's wife said she heard one calling out from inside, as if through a tunnel. The farmer digs a hole to bury Magic with his tractor. I pull on my jacket and head out to feed the motherless kid.

How Cruel the World

Twinkle bawls incessantly, only stopping when I stroke her. The loss she feels. New to the milk stand, new to this pasture—a yearling reared a mile off at Hollow Road. I remember walking home from the library alone on Crete, nine years old, in tears, just having read *The Yearling*. After dumping the muck, I hug Twinkle. Life sucks sometimes, I tell her.

I'm in trouble; missed a snowy market day, didn't mark my calendar. Stressful and exasperating, the farm owner's wife called it.

How easily I could lose this barn, these goats. I don't want to think about all the additional adoption paperwork, my money leaking like milk from swollen teats. Some would say cheese is a bestiality one embraces, so as to live out loud, animally. Others would have animal ethics include the right to an unsupervised sexual life and parenthood. Yes, I wonder what I'm doing, Twinkle. I have made it to middle age childless. Who can aid us in our hormonal suffering?

The Gardener

A goat cries incessantly. My dog answers in gruff reply. Behind the barn, a gardener whacks weeds. His hands are dark with earth as I hand him ice water.

Bark Peeled

The deer have eaten bark off the vine-choked tree down near the creek that snakes through the eight-acre farm. The dog is giddy, running through muck. Skunk cabbage shoots up. Yesterday I cried because again I've found myself attracted to a man who cannot father.

True Temper

So much depends upon the pissy farm owner who fingers the straw in my wheelbarrow and tells me to be more careful when shoveling manure. In the mail: a bill for adoption, but still no promise of a child. The key bends as I try to open my truck door. I don't have a spare. And now there is the curse of grass: a circle the farm owner's wife spray paints and I dig. Her self-importance. My muscles. And the wheelbarrow and spade stamped 'True Temper.'

The Trial

I lost it and began screaming. I was cleaning the kids' stall that reeked of ammonia. Stop, I screamed. Stop.

Fifi stopped her screaming, but only for a second, surprised. She'd been at it for hours, her cries resounding off concrete floors of the old, thick-walled stable. Her kid had been taken from her, I learned later, and immediately regretted the noise I'd made, the switch that was flipped in my own hurt self, hearing her go on and on.

The End of Labor

I ready the farm owner's wife's soil, digging her garden for her as she sits inside her stone house and writes her bestseller about how to farm. The difference between overseeing and doing is often the difference between writing and life. In America, writing is something done for fame, or at least for money. It requires an agent—I can't do this myself, is what the farm owner's wife says—and consumers hungry to learn how to manage their own million-dollar farms. If I sound bitter about the publishing industry, or about my labor that will never be enough to procure me a farm or perhaps even a child, I hope you'll hear me out as I insist that writing still matters, that doing and being with goats has taught me to look for words that do not pad the matter. Life is bleak, life is barren, even this spring with all the kids nestled in their pens. I must leave this tenant life. I do not know where I'll go, but that is not the issue. The issue is what it means to say: I was here, I labored.

A Short History of the White Gaze

Hilton Als's essay 'GWTW'—a preface to *Without Sanctuary*, a collection of photographs of North American lynchings—resurfaced in my consciousness as I was watching Steve McQueen's *12 Years a Slave* in the theater the other evening. I had gone to see the film, so as to participate in a roundtable discussion. After the film let out, Cherise, a colleague, spoke loudly and without affect in a bathroom filled with weepy white women. I was one of those weepy white women. And although I was not in the mood to eat or drink anything, I accompanied Cherise to the theater's café. There we spoke about the film: she, about decisions McQueen made at the expense of black women's bodies, especially his decision, in the first scene, to throw a desirous woman onto Northup and to then flashback to Northrup and his wife, and I, about the war on terror and what it means to look at images of torture—be they fictional or real, or based upon the real.

Much has already been made of the liberties McQueen took translating Solomon Northup's autobiography to the screen. Similarly, scholarship already exists on how the film's artifice is only one of a series of removes that begin with the question of representational accuracy of Northup's dictated autobiography, written down and arranged by David Wilson, a white lawyer from Glens Falls, New York, who fit Northup's tale within a certain narrative structure. But McQueen's refusal to treat slavery as a fictional genre and to instead insist upon its truth by largely staying true to the corroborated autobiographical elements of Northrup's life demands viewers face the music: slavery is real, it happened, this film is not entertainment.

In fact, I find myself revisiting Hilton Als's question of why anyone would want to look at images of lynching now, precisely because McQueen's film is a representation of the real. In his classic essay that accompanies the collection of lynching photographs, *Without Sanctuary* (edited mostly by white persons), Als questions the usefulness of the book (which he refers to as a collection of photographs, which, 'when viewed together, make up America's first disaster movie'), as, he argues, he identifies with the lynched and with being a subject of the white gaze. But who, Als asks in this essay, do white people identify with while looking at these images: the maimed, the tortured, the dead, or the white people?

Let me turn the question on myself: with whom do I identify in *12 Years a Slave*? I surprise myself with my answer: I identify with everyone—all the actors and actresses, and I also identify with those doing the shooting and even with McQueen and Northup and David Wilson. What does such extreme white mimicry do for anyone? I know the dangers of such mimicry; I know that it can make me self-identify as non-white and in doing so help me blissfully and wrongly forget what my whiteness grants. But might such empathy also teach me (a once white fourteen-year-old auditioning on my high school stage by playing all the parts to a script that was by no means a monologue) something? Might this over-identification be a form of self-punishment that a white person must pass through in order to emerge a still blind, but apprenticing anti-racist?

Perhaps. But definitely, beyond identifying, a white person must also account for his or her gaze as a perpetrator or bystander of lynchings and beatings and other tortures (regardless whether contemplating the real or representations of the real), as one is complicit regardless. So the question becomes: how do I stand it? How can I just sit there watching torture happen? I still remember a story I was told when I was a young girl about an old Western that was shown in Tibet and how a Tibetan in the audience, who had never before seen a moving picture, shot the cowboy in the film— literally shot the screen. This conflation of truth and fiction is the essence of McQueen's film. This is why I find myself wrestling with the feeling that I now have to *do* something.

Before I get ahead of myself, let me rewind to the fictionalized scene in which a recently caught slave on board the ship with Northup attempts to thwart a slaver on his way to rape another slave and is stabbed. (According to Northup's account, the stabbing didn't happen.) This man's body is then cast overboard, as it was in Northup's account when a man named Robert died of smallpox. Northup states in his memoir:

> It was soon announced that he had the small-pox. He continued to grow worse, and four days previous to our arrival in New-Orleans he died. One of the sailors sewed him in his blanket, with a large stone from the ballast at his feet, and then laying him on a hatch-

way, and elevating it with tackles above the railing, the inanimate body of poor Robert was consigned to the white waters of the gulf.

Watching the body—or in this filmic representation whatever prop was used—sink, I couldn't help but think of the sea burial the U.S. military gave Osama bin Laden after the U.S. Navy SEALS murdered the man without solid evidence that proved beyond doubt he was linked to the 9/11 bombings. Evidence is the key word here, in that evidence is still lacking, no trial was given, and none will be had (as if a person of color could ever trust due process, anyway, in any predominantly white man's court). Evidence is also what photographs of the real and films based on reality expose or invoke. *Without Sanctuary* and *12 Years a Slave* serve as varying forms of evidence of the horrible injustice historically done unto persons of color by white persons. And it is worth mentioning again that while watching *12 Years a Slave*, I couldn't help but think of how the U.S. military continues to exploit, torture, and kill persons of color—be they Yemeni Americans, African Americans, Libyans, Iraqis, Afghanis, Somalis, you name it—in the most unjust of ways.

A few years ago, Howard E. Wasdin came out with a book (with Stephen Templin) *SEAL Team Six* about his U.S. Navy SEAL days in which he makes killing sound like taking a picture: an exercise in determining the distance of oneself from one's subject. 'I calculated the exact distances to certain buildings,' Wasdin writes.

> There are two primary considerations when making a sniper shot, windage and elevation. Because there was no significant wind that could throw my shot left or right, I didn't have to compensate for it... I still didn't know if I'd hit the target or not. It's not like the movies, where the shot disintegrates the target. In reality the bullet goes through the body so fast that sometimes people don't even realize they've been shot...

Wasdin's distance is not as technical as it is clinical. How does one become such a calculating murderer, and then live freely to brag about it?

It was the SEAL Team Six who shot bin Laden through the head. And speaking of evidence: no pictures of bin Laden's murder were ever released to the public. 'We don't trot this stuff out as trophies,' President Obama told *CBS*. Evidence, in this case, is not trophy; it is what holds a nation accountable for its crimes against humanity.

Regardless who looks at such images and for what reasons, these images are of use beyond the trophy, as these images also accuse. History sides with those who have been wronged. This is why I look at images of torture. They remind me, as do memoirs written by the tortured and enslaved, that the human condition needs constant abolitionist, anti-imperialist attention.

Consider Mohamedou Ould Slahi's memoir, *Guantánamo Diary*. Slahi (who the CIA, the FBI, and military intelligence have not been able to connect with any links to terrorism and who is still imprisoned at Guantánamo) herein writes of being subjected to months of 20-hour-a-day interrogations. He writes of detainees being hanged by the hands: 'The punishment for talking was hanging the detainee by his hands with the feet barely touching the ground... Most of the detainees tried to talk while hanging, which makes the guards double their punishment...' He writes of being sexually tortured:

> As soon as I stood up, the two [redacted] took off their blouses and started to talk all kinds of dirty stuff you can imagine. Both [redacted] stuck on me literally from the front, and the other older [redacted] stuck on my back, rubbing [redacted] whole body on mine. At the same time they were talking dirty to me, and playing with my sexual parts...from noon or before until 10 p.m.

And he writes of being subjected to a mock rendition:

> Suddenly a commando team of three soldiers and a German shepherd broke into our interrogation room. [Redacted] punched me violently, which made me fall face down on the floor, and the second guy kept punching me everywhere, mainly on my face and my ribs. Both were masked from head to toe... My first thought was, they mistook me for somebody else. My second thought was to try to look around, but one of the guards was squeezing my face against the floor. I saw the dog fighting to get loose... 'Blindfold the motherfucker! He's trying to look—' One of them hit me hard across the face and quickly put goggles on my eyes, earmuffs on my ears, and a small bag over my head. They tightened the chains around my ankles and my wrists; afterward I started to bleed. All I could hear was [Redacted] cursing, 'F-ing this and F-ing that.' I thought they were going to execute me.

During this torture session, someone sprayed ammonia in Slahi's nose to keep him from passing out, and, after being trucked to a beach, an escort team placed the victim in a high-speed boat and took him for a three-hour ride around the Caribbean, then fastened him to a chair, and, as Slahi writes,

> stuffed the air between my clothes and me with ice cubes from my neck to my ankles, and whenever the ice melted they put in new hard ice cubes. Moreover, every once in a while, one of the guards smashed me, most of the time in the face. The ice served both for pain and for wiping out the bruises I had from that afternoon. Everything seemed to be perfectly prepared. Historically, dictators during medieval and pre-medieval times used this method to let the victim die slowly. The other method of hitting the victim while blindfolded in inconsistent intervals of time was used by Nazis during WWII. There is nothing more terrorizing than making somebody expect a smash every single heartbeat...

I excerpt Slahi's memoir at length, because it needs placing next to Als's 'GWTW' and McQueen's *12 Years a Slave* as a real document that testifies to the ongoingness of North American perpetrated injustices. War reporter Michael Hirsh puts it this way:

> On the most simplistic level the film [*12 Years a Slave*] is the ultimate antidote to *Gone with the Wind* and the persistent pretensions of an American South that, despite 150 years of fitful racial progress, still tends to glorify its irredeemably shameful past in culture, word, and song. But the real meaning of the film [*12 Years a Slave*] transcends the problem of slavery and the undercurrent of racism that continues to afflict our country today... The larger theme, rendered with great artistry, is what happens when a helpless people is subjugated by a greater force with no accountability. It is, in other words, not just about what it's like to be a slave but also what it's like to be part of an often brutal occupation by a superpower.

If a war apologist like Hirsh can see history repeating itself, perhaps I am preaching to the choir. If not, please make more of an effort to be less entertained by this film. We need a present society that is watchful—not one that gazes fearfully and hatefully, without seeing or feeling.

How to be more present, more mindful, Zadie Smith asks, while reviewing several books by Karl Ove Knausgaard and Tao Lin's *Taipei*. In this same review Smith mentions that Americans viewed twelve times as many Web pages about Miley Cyrus as about the gas attack in Syria, then implicates her own self by confessing, 'I read plenty about Miley Cyrus, on my iPhone, late at night. And you wake up and you hate yourself...'

In this review, Smith also tries to identify with the corpse in a drawing by Luca Signorelli. 'Not only does my imagination quail at the prospect of imagining myself a corpse,' Smith writes, 'even my eyes cannot be faithful to the corpse for long, drawn back instead to the monumental vigor. To the back and buttocks, the calves, the arms. Across the chasms of gender, color, history, and muscle definition, I am the man and the man is me. Oh, I can very easily imagine carrying a corpse! See myself hulking it some distance... Corpses,' she continues, 'spring flower-like in budded clusters whenever a bomb goes off in the marketplaces of Iraq and Afghanistan.'

A corpse isn't what Smith wants to imagine she will become, but if she must imagine it, she reveals, she would then want to live a worthy life and begin to do so by throwing away her iPhone. No matter the state of Smith's present cell phone, her review, 'Man vs. Corpse,' is about realism, the banal, and how Ove Knausgaard and Lin rely not on metaphor, beauty, or drama, but are fully present authors who document life in every detail, blow-by-blow, without affect, as if the writing and the living are happening simultaneously and, even though nothing happens in these authors' books, the banal struggle is both intolerable and beautiful because it is real.

In many respects Slahi's memoir of torture, Als's 'GWTW,' and McQueen's filmic portrayal of Northup's slave narrative are similarly intolerable, fully present, and horrifyingly beautiful documents. I will also argue that these documents are even more real than the banal fictional and artistic struggles documented in the works Smith describes (which appeal to the crowd with whom Smith hangs: Hal Foster and the elite of New York's art and literary scene).

Often these days, when I'm struggling to write, I find myself wondering out loud whether I should abandon the essayistic and nonfiction genre for a fictional one. It would be easier, I argue. But whenever I think about what would happen to the material with which I work, material that is so hot (for it is *true*) it regularly burns my psyche, I throw myself back at the world of the real. I cannot abandon Slahi. Similarly Northup's tale is real and the truth of McQueen's video cannot be escaped. Fiction equals distance, and distance keeps us less than present, if not pleasantly anaes-thetized.

Let me end by erasing the distance between others' representa-tions of the real and the reality I live. Like Slahi, I am childless and this is my weakest point. Slahi's torturers found this weakness and exploited it by placing photographs of cribs around his interrogation room and mock-ing his lack of manliness. I have been attempting to adopt and ethically struggling with the process—primarily with what it means to be white and pay money, so as to facilitate an adoption. Such agreements formed the beginnings of colonialism and slavery. In McQueen's film, we witness the selling of children, the splitting of them from their mother Eliza, and Eliza's subsequent unraveling. We witness Northup's anger at Eliza's tears, and her accusation of his own hard-heartedness. In Northup's memoir, Eliza's grief is equally unnerving. Northup relates:

> never have I seen such an exhibition of intense, unmeasured, and unbounded grief, as when Eliza was parted from her child. She broke from her place in the line of women, and rushing down where Emily was standing, caught her in her arms. The child, sen-sible of some impending danger, instinctively fastened her hands around her mother's neck, and nestled her little head upon her bo-som. Freeman sternly ordered her to be quiet, but she did not heed him. He caught her by the arm and pulled her rudely, but she only clung the closer to the child. Then, with a volley of great oaths, he struck her such a heartless blow, that she staggered backward, and was like to fall. Oh! how piteously then did she beseech and beg and pray that they might not be separated. Why could they not be purchased together? Why not let her have one of her dear children? 'Mercy, mercy, master!' she cried, falling on her knees. 'Please, master, buy Emily. I can never work any if she is taken from me: I will die.'

Northup tells us that Eliza never sees or hears of her children again. 'Day nor night, however, were they ever absent from her memory,' he relates. 'In the cotton field, in the cabin, always and everywhere, she was talking of them—often to them, as if they were actually present...'

When I speak on the phone with my friend and she pushes me to articulate why I am so conflicted about the adoption process, I prickle. Why am I so set on parenting a child of color? This is her question. It is actually her mother's question. I do not know how to answer. Is it a hatred of my own race, a racist glorification of another, white guilt, historical violence unconsciously repeated, economic constraints (as children of color cost less to adopt than white children), or all of the above? And why is it that I see myself within the photographs of children of color on the waiting children photolistings? What is it I see? in me or them? in these texts? The fact is that I am attempting to escape my own reality. I do not want to be childless and I do not want to own my whiteness. I want to fling it like a mask into the bushes. Am I really the white mistress, Mistress Epps, so jealous she cuts the face of Patsey—the slave who picks more than 500 pounds of cotton a day—and then urges her husband (who rapes and slaps Patsey at night) to whip Patsey until she's too bloody to stand, and who, in Northup's account, bribes Northup to kill Patsey? If I am Mistress Epps, I have to die.

I keep coming back to being wrong, I tell April.

Sure, she says, we're all wrong, but we're loved and we can always try to be better.

Does this mean Mistress Epps can learn? She's dead, but simply asking myself this question does something to me. It frees me a little. You have to forgive yourself, April is saying. You have to do this before any little body comes into your life.

Nobody's going to come into my life, I respond defensively, but I'm thinking: forgive Mistress Epps? It seems entirely impossible, yet I know that civil rights and anti-apartheid movements were built on nothing less.

I have to forgive all the slights, all those failings brought on by my whiteness, where I have been blind and hurt others, and selfish and hurt others, and I have to open myself and accept this self. I have to read and watch and feel the horrific lust and fear and hatred inside those with power and acknowledge it all within myself. If Smith can identify with a corpse, then I can identify with the slave owner's wife, the torturer.

At a certain point in 'GWTW,' Als states that he will never again write such a piece as one that forces him to acknowledge the triteness of language, the way he has become 'a cliché, another colored person writing about a nigger's life.' For a long while, Als admits, he rejected black nationalism's limits—that is until he realized that such limits were imposed not by black nationalism but by white supremacy.

Perhaps the thing I can do, the most useful thing at this moment, albeit cliché, is to turn the gaze away from the lynching and honestly level my eyes at myself. Who am I sitting here, typing on this snow-bound evening in Pennsylvania? Who am I but white hands on a black keyboard? I want to turn the attention away from me to the dog behind me, her mass curled beneath a felt blanket. I want not to sit here, uncomfortably, in the midst of my banal comforts, my loneliness, my silence, my whiteness. How do I hold myself accountable as a childless 41-year-old who still yearns to become a mom?

It was never my sole intent to adopt a child of color. It is what I began to orient myself toward given my circumstances as a single, poor person. Yet now that I know how rife with racial tensions and cultural misunderstandings the adoption and foster care network is, what do I *do*? How to hold adoption and child-welfare legislation more accountable for race, class, and cultural concerns? How, for example, to help immigrants who lose their children to North American adoptive families regain custody of their children? And how to hold this white self accountable—especially in light of past NAACP legislation that decreed white parents unable to respectfully rear children of color in North America? Is the answer to give up, remain childless? adopt white? Ultimately, of course, the answer is to fight against racism, poverty, and disease, and for affordable care, education, and human and environmental rights for all persons. I *do* this. And I still hope beyond hope that I can find the loop-hole, the right way to be white, the right way to become a parent, and the right way to raise a child— most likely (given my circumstances and the world's) a child of color.

A Short History of the Black Impulse to See

Makula

An African family in a sparklingly modern interior in Léopoldville, Belgian Congo, sits around the dining room table, engaged in conversation. A refrigerator, a set of comfortable chairs, and framed art on the kitchen wall bedeck the scene. The father in his starched and ironed dress shirt commands attention at the head of the table. The children sit, backs to the camera. The mother smiles, her white dress's neck cut in a seashell scoop. Joseph Makula, the Congolese photographer for the newspaper *Sango ya Biso*, showcases the Congolese upper class, poised are they are to upend the colonial state.

Parks

Gordon Parks's photographs in the 1956 *Life Magazine* essay 'The Restraints: Open and Hidden' are documentary in style, shot in color, and cover a twelve-page spread. The photo essay begins with a shot of Mr. and Mrs. Albert Thornton, aged 82 and 70, on a couch in their living room. Mr. Thornton is dressed in shirt and tie, and Mrs. Thornton in a flowered dress, hands crossed in her lap. The couple stare directly at the photographer. A wedding photograph hangs above them on the wall made from separate portraits, taken respectively in 1903, and spliced together. Mr. Thornton, the son of a slave, was once a sharecropper, and is pictured in Parks's essay leading his cows to pasture and walking his grandchildren down a dirt road. Cutlines inform the viewer that none of the roads where the Thorntons live is paved and that erosion from the rains has caused neighborhood houses to tilt and splay.

This photo essay illustrates other challenges of segregation: we see the Thornton children outside a fenced playground watching white children enjoy themselves. We also are shown segregated water fountains and waiting areas, and signs for 'colored lots for sale.' All the while, Parks portrays the family with the same dignity with which the members of this family carry themselves.

Keita

I respect how Seydou Keita poses others, how he photographs. His is a humane venture. Why? Let me begin with his image of three men. Two wear brimmed hats. All are outfitted in their best—an eclectic mix of dress shirts and slacks. Each sitter has his own style. One has donned a patterned tie; another wears a zippered sweater. Their faces aren't those of city slickers; they look hardened, resigned. Yet they are young, their eyes still inquire as they look to the lens. They look, but do not allow their gaze to be returned by just anyone. This photograph wasn't taken for, or by, a stranger—these men asked and paid for it. They wanted a reminder of themselves.

In this photograph I see another: August Sander's *Three Young Farmers*. The men Keita photographs, however, look other than those Sander pictures. Study the men's expressions. Sander's farmers' smirks and almost cocky poses blatantly contrast Keita's sitters' inward-turned, self-possessed expressions. As it happened, Sander was roaming the countryside when he came across his young farmers on their way to a dance. Granted, the farmers were happy to pose, but they were not seeking his gaze. In contrast, the men in Keita's studio established a relationship with Keita. Because they approached him, requesting he make their portrait, they are fully present, and in control of the production of their own history.

Although Keita's negatives (he kept them all in case a sitter ever wanted another copy printed) are presently out of both the sitters' and Keita's posthumous control, thanks to the international art market, the way the images were made cannot be wrested so easily from their original social contract. Keita's photographs (like those of other Malian photographers who established their own studios in Bamako during French Colonial rule and began to make portraits that bespoke a postcolonial African identity even before Malian independence) will always speak of both the sitters' and photographer's attempt to portray the sitters' ideal selves.

When photographing, Keita paid attention to which eye to award what light and which limb to foreground. He used depth of field to situate, render. The patterns of his backdrops compliment patterns worn by his customers, highlighting and accenting their forms. His first backdrop was a bed-cover. Later, he changed the backdrop every two or three years. 'Sometimes the backdrop went well with the clothes, especially the women's clothes,' he told André Magnin in 1994. 'But that was just luck.' What luck!

His compositions depend upon sitters' gestures, costumes, and props, but his images are other than those produced in other portrait shops in Mali at this time, largely because of his genius use of available light. Compare Keita's shots with Malik Sidibe's portraits and note the difference Sidibe's harsh flash makes; Keita preferred not to indulge his sitters' requests for night photos that, because of the flash, made their skin appear lighter.

Keita not only pointed his camera at his sitters, he worked to complete the frame to best fulfill his sitters' wishes. The sitters were his customers; he wanted to satisfy and put bread on his table. He wasn't interested in photography as appropriation; he loved it as a functional art, yet he was also an artist invested in reproducing the postcolonial black man and woman as he saw fit. 'Clients would say: I want to be photographed like that, you see? That's what I want. And that's what I'd do,' Kieta told Magnin.

But sometimes it didn't suit them at all. I would suggest a position which would suit them better, and then it was I who decided on the right position, I was always spot on. It took me just a few minutes, no more. A lot of clients came along, but Saturdays were best; sometimes there were over a hundred. At times there was even a queue. Well off people, mostly civil servants and tradesmen. Even the first President of Mali came...

Regardless his cliental, Keita's eye was always egalitarian. Two years after Mali's independence, Keita became the photographer for the new socialist government and shut down his studio. Later, under the Traore dictatorship, he abandoned his post and became a mechanic.

Whereas Sander photographed to typify (the quintessential baker, brick-layer, Nazi), his scientific lens in grim service to an idea of a total humanity rather than to those who posed for him, Keita's images speak of a relationship between the photographer and the photographed, of what it means to work together.

Fosso and Shinobare

Samuel Fosso began breaking with the African studio tradition of portraiture and playing dress up and photographing himself after fleeing the Biafran war and working as a photographer's assistant in the Central African Republic. In one of his famous self-portraits, he dresses as a femme fatale; in another, he wears a golfer's attire. In the photograph Fosso likes best, he wears rectangular white glasses, jewelry, holds a bouquet of sunflowers, and is scantily clad in leopard-print, regal attire. A pair of red dress shoes rest beside the leopard-print covered chair on which he sits, feet bare, the surrounding floor and walls draped in colorful African cloth. About the image, Fosso states: 'I am all the African chiefs who have sold their continent to the white men... [W]e had our own systems, our own rulers, before you came.'

Yinka Shonibare pushes Fosso's dandyism to another level with his photographic series *Diary of a Victorian Dandy*. Here is Shonibare spread-eagled in a Victorian room on a period couch, clothed in a pink double-breasted vest coat, a pink tie, and black trousers. White women drape themselves all over him, each one clothed in a white petticoat. Shonibare is the centerpiece of this orgy. Behind him and to the side, white men grope white women and white women grope; others just look on. Throughout the series, Shonibare holds forth, the only black in the room. Whether he is referencing a passage in a book he holds open, playing pool, or convalescing, he commands the gaze. Of course, the British Empire was built on the back of slaves, which only serves to underline the rarity of such a dandy and heighten the punch of Shonibare's photographs.

Compare, if you will, Fosso's and Shonibare's African dandy with Baudelaire's—a man with no occupation but to chase happiness; a man habituated to being obeyed with no profession other than elegance, free to cultivate the idea of beauty and translate fantasy into reality. As evidenced by the work of Fosso and Shonibare, the African dandy does not adhere to such Western definition; rather, the African dandy critiques dandyism even as he performs it.

Weems

Traveling through South Carolina and Georgia, where slaves were sold after a torturous crossing of the Atlantic and where the Gullah-Geechee people (descendants of freed slaves) managed to salvage much of their African and Creole cultural heritages, Carrie Mae Weems embarks on photographing postmemory—the memory of trauma she herself did not experience, but which has been passed down to her epigenetically. She protects herself by photographing how those before her protected themselves: mattress springs in trees to stop evil spirits from flying; window frames painted blue to dissuade evil spirits from entering; a bowl of water placed outside the door to be tossed after the evil spirits have exited.

Mthethwa (before)

Zwelethu Mthethwa's portraits of poor, mostly black South Africans echo Walker Evans's shots of poor white Southerners. Mthethwa and Evans portray the poor as decent folk. Words like dignified and defiant have been used to describe what these men's cameras elicit from their subjects. Differences in time, place, and race between the two photographers attest to the similar *and* opposing approaches each employ. Evans's frontal portraiture is now considered a typified, canonical framing of poverty. Mthethwa also encounters his subjects face on. Like Evans, Mthethwa goes in search of his subjects and waits for them to invite him in. He gives sitters time to present themselves and promises them prints. But while Evans belonged to the time of black and white photography, Mthethwa embraces Kodachrome, as, he says that he can't ignore the importance of color in his subject's homes. 'They try,' he adds, 'with the little that they have, to make their homes colorful, highly intentioned, beautiful. If you convert the images [that I make] into black and white there is nothing there to see except poverty. It would look like a political campaign.'

Take away the color in Mthethwa's work and the housing conditions of the contemporary poor South Africans in Mthethwa's images are as spare as the Depression-era shacks of the 1930s North American South. Mthethwa's portraits of agricultural workers, however, take color to another level: the green of the fields is almost unreal and the harvested hills that dip and rise into thin air serve as stark contrast to the muscled men dressed in black gum boots and faded, torn sweaters. In black and white, these photographs would relegate these people and their work to the past. Mthethwa's images do the opposite—they impose with their very live color and scale (printed life-size), announcing their place, taking up space, refusing to be relegated to the back of any gallery.

Mthethwa, the first black to graduate from the Michaelis School of Fine Art in Cape Town, unflinchingly records the socio-economic reality of blacks in post-apartheid South Africa where almost half the population is unemployed and one in four live in shacks without water or electricity. Standing before Mthethwa's photos, it is impossible to dismiss men who must wear layer upon layer of clothes to protect themselves from the barbed stalks and snakes, or to disregard the women who chip away at bricks in a city's ruins, recycling material for future use. The message is clear: the poor continue to shoulder the burden of making the world from scratch.

Mthethwa (after)

Found guilty of kicking a 23-year-old sex worker to death, Zwelethu Mthethwa is locked up. His photographs are difficult now for me to embrace. I did love them. I did find his approach sensitive. I thought he gave his sitters time to arrange themselves. But all I see today is the green of the fields that are almost unreal and the harvested hills that dip and rise into thin air—fields I learned belong to Mthethwa's family. It is his parents who employ the workers in their tattered sweaters and gumboots. The silence of the photographs is broken by the sound of Mthethwa's special order black Porsche as it speeds away from Nokuphila Kumalo's ravaged, lifeless body. He beat her so severely one of her eyes is still missing.

Muholi

I don't complain anymore, I make things happen, Zanele Muholi says.

She is at Yale, behind a podium, dressed in a T-shirt, a bowler hat, and colorful sneakers, speaking about how, as a young South African, she found no images that reflected her own reality. 'I work with participants, not subjects,' she says, underlining the importance of how she meets those she photographs: through friends. Muholi talks on about Inkanyisu, an organization she created that ensures participants can also obtain access to a camera to document their own lives. Then she brings up the funerals. 'Her head was crushed with a big stone. Her teeth were all over the place,' Muholi says of Noxolo Nogwaza who was raped, stoned, and stabbed in KwaThema, Guateng. 'We all documented that lesbian funeral; every person who had a cell phone with a camera. We downloaded and shared. Made that document viral.'

Mahashe films in the backseat of the Mercedes taxi en route to Doula, Cameroon. He's collecting a stream of African street scenes. 'If you can't win the war against images, maybe it is time,' he tells me, 'to do away with images.'

We've been talking about neocolonialism, the archive, and what's at stake when it comes to African photography. George Mahashe is from Bolobedu at Ga-kgapane, South Africa. He just wanted to photograph his hometown women beer drinkers but was accused by his professors at the University of Capetown of perpetuating the colonial gaze. Ever since, he has been liberating colonial images from the archive, making copies for people to steal, and encouraging high school students to engage with the images and begin conversations about them with their grandparents.

George is going to Douala to see a Samuel Fosso show. I have to fly back to the States.

I email him a week later, requesting to teach his work in a seminar and sending him the syllabus in which I quote Audre Lorde's question of whether one can ever dismantle the master's house with the master's tools. 'Are these really the master's tools?' George emails back, adding:

> In my work I have become interested in understanding the tools as things that existed in different ways across time (before the master), which have been reconfigured by the 'master' at a specific time for specific reasons... I have become interested in understanding both the...impulse to see, epitomized in the idea of the camera, and in understanding...how the rise of the photograph...came to be the central apparatus [through which]...the 'master' lays claim to the world.

A Short History of Insect Lessons

Pregnant female gnats are the ones that hunger after the protein in our sweat, tears, pus, and blood. But all gnats are called *pusio*, meaning 'little boy.' The *pusio* belongs to the order *Diptera*, 'two wings,' and to the family *Chloropidae*, 'swarm,' and to the genus *Liohippelates*, 'horse drivers.' Ever since Socrates defended himself against charges of corrupting Athenian youth by comparing himself to a gadfly (of the order *Diptera*) bothering a lazy horse,[1] insects have become metaphors of the hard path to justice. Easy to swat, yet ever-burrowing into the body of the polis, the cost to society of silencing such bother is high.

As a young man, my father attempted to whip the populace into fury. After driving Reverend James Reeb from Atlanta to Selma, Alabama, where Reeb was beaten by white racists, my father wrote a letter to the government that began: 'They say [Reeb]...is going to die tonight and I'm kind of wondering what, if he dies, we can say he died for.' By the end of the letter, my father conceded that he would refuse to continue to work within the establishment for change, for it was the establishment itself he was fighting.

Whereas Socrates believed that bothering the polis would expose what he referred to as 'divine truth,' Walter Benjamin believed that the path to justice would come about through what he called 'divine violence.' 'Divine violence' was, Benjamin proposed, opposed to lawmaking which invoked guilt and retribution. Rather, 'divine violence' was law-destroying in that it only forgave. Nonviolent action depended upon laws, Benjamin reasoned, and laws always led to violence, as they conferred on each party the right to resort to violence in some form against the other, should any one party break the agreement.

---

[1] The pregnant gadfly dive-bombs the horse, so as to lay its eggs atop of the inside flesh of its flanks. The horse then scratches and licks the eggs, thereby transferring the parasitic larvae to its gastrointestinal track. Without treatment, such flies can kill a horse.

About a decade before my father drove Reeb to Selma, where Reeb died two days after being beaten, Torkel Weis-Fogh and August Krogh tethered a locust to measure how heavily it breathed as it flew. The observations made by this zoologist and respiration physiologist (who believed that for any problem an animal could be studied to solve it) were immediately embraced as the preeminent theory on insect flight. Weis-Fogh's and Krogh's clap-and-fling effect maintains that insects' wing motions create low-pressure pockets that then refill with air, creating a swirling, tornado-shaped vortex that the wing then slices as it pulls a faster stream of air up into the vortex. The angle of the wing as it hits the wake capture[2] is what provides the insect with downward or upward force.[3] Force, created by wing movement, is perhaps a type of 'divine violence,' in that it appeals to no law. In fact, even though insects make up 80 percent of the planet's animal species, little has ever been understood about how they keep themselves aloft. The wings of bees, for example, lift more weight than can be explained by steady-state aerodynamics.[4]

I knew little about steady-state aerodynamics the day the married man came over and sat beside me in the grass behind a colleague's condo. His gesture, it struck me then, was a generous one, as generous as the yard was long, all the backs of the condos the same. I don't know how I ended up here, I told this man. I was speaking both of academia and of the development.

     Neither do I, he said.

Expectation is a black hole, a vortex, in which a certain amount of energy swirls around one spot, not unlike how water swirls in one direction in the toilet bowl on one side of the equator and in the other direction on the other. Whichever side of the energy swirl one is on determines, I believe, a large portion of whatever will happen next. Yet expectations are usually,

---

[2] A 'wake capture' is the collision of the air stream with the vortex.
[3] Most wing movements create waves of vortices that merge and build. The resulting sound is the insect's buzz.
[4] According to steady-state aerodynamics, the sum of lift and weight as well as thrust and drag all must equal zero, as there can be no imbalance of such forces in steady, straight flight.

in my book, not about ending up with anything, or even about what's real. Expectations are actually, I've found, not about what might happen, but about narrative, poem, the folding of words into forms that tend to break the surface of things to show us the bigger picture, not only our own particular speck. Words create something other than what is—they create an alternative, no matter how real I might wish they were. And this was why I like them. I find their approximation beautiful.

This, too, was how I felt sitting next to the married man.

Some years after the insect flight paper was published, Weis-Fogh's student, Charles Ellington, built a robotic approximation of a hawkmoth's wing, placed it in a smoke-filled tunnel to visually analyze its fluid dynamics, and noted a leading-edge vortex spiraling out along the moth's down-stroked wingtip. The wingtip, Ellington discovered, had a spanwise velocity comparable to a flapping velocity. In fact, the vortex was so intense in force it basically lifted the moth upward. Ellington's study inspired Rob Wood who worked for the next seven years to mechanically replicate a fruit fly's wing, and then labored another five to replicate its flight, all the while studying videos and images captured at 7,500 frames per second. Wood was most fascinated by how flies collided with glass. They hit legs-first, he found, wings stopping momentarily. Before recovering, they dropped in the air and glided a bit. It was only a matter of time before Wood fashioned carbon fiber and plastic shock absorbers for the legs of the world's first drone.

A plethora of micro-drones modeled after insects now take off and land practically anywhere, turn on a dime, and kill with the click of a mouse. There are Dragonfly drones, Black Hornet Nano drones, Spy-butterfly drones, Roachbot drones, Mosquito drones that can draw someone's DNA, and it all started with a tethered locust.[5]

Drones have become nearly as common as insects in North Waziristan, Pakistan, a poor border-region from which the U.S. once recruited men to fight the Russians. As many as six are said to hover over any particular village at any given time, whirring and firing unpredictably. Parents do

---

[5] The Defense Advanced Research Projects Agency (DARPA) now even implants electro-mechanical chips into live insects, mounts them with cameras, and flies them wherever the government wishes.

not trust that their children will return from school alive and families are afraid to attend funerals for fear they will be gunned down by these un-manned aircrafts. Pakistan's newspaper *The News*, reported that between January 14, 2006, and April 8, 2009, sixty drone attacks killed 701 peo-ple, 14 of whom were militants. Drones are said to be silent, but reports out of Pakistan state that drones produce a monotonous buzz, almost like the sound of a generator. Particularly affected, one report reads, are young children who are said to be unable to sleep at night and cry due to the noise. Forty-five thousand Pakistanis have thus far lost their lives to U.S. drone strikes in Waziristan.

Martin Luther King once said, 'Justice denied anywhere diminishes justice everywhere,' and sure enough, wherever drones congregate, suicide bomb-ers spring up in their shadow. Our nation, however, continues to tell itself its own holier than thou moral lies. Such lies, not unlike the construction of race as identity, are mere myths, but the reality accompanying their in-terpretation is anything but. Crimes committed do not disappear. Memory is identity.

On the website that accompanies Maya Lin's newest installation, a swarm of lights turns from constellations of animals into flocks of birds into lights of cities, as Lin memorializes species loss. Click on any city light and a frag-ment of such loss appears. I click, and the passenger pigeon alights. A pen and ink drawing of the bird appears, beside which is posted the following (from a speech at an 1815 Audubon Society meeting):

> The destruction of the wild pigeon...has meant a loss as severe as if the Catskills of the Palisades were taken away. When I hear of the destruction of the species, I feel just as if all the works of some great writer had perished, as if we had lost all instead of only a part...

I haven't experienced it myself, but I've read that Lin's physical memorial includes a sound installation, or listening cone, that plays recordings of endangered or already extinct species. These calls of birds and frogs and whales, like indigenous languages that are also being lost, might never—and in many cases won't ever—be heard in the wild again.

There is no central list of existing species on the planet because they are dying faster than we care to count. Biologists estimate that there are between five million and ten million species in total, but studies suggest there are many more. In the 1970s, a researcher in Panama counted beetle species living in a single tree and found 1,100 species of which 160 depended solely upon that particular tree for survival. With 50,000 known tropical tree species (out of a total of 100,000 known tree species in the world), this researcher estimated that there were at least 160 beetle species exclusive to each tropical tree, and guessed the number of beetle species in tropical forests alone was at least eight million. But the researcher was only counting the beetles in the trees' canopies. Colin Tudge points out that there are half as many more beetles living in tree roots and surrounding soil, so his guess is that there could be as many as 30 million beetle species just in tropical forests. Then, too, he surmises, there are even smaller species like parasites (of which there is one for each beetle), and mites that live on parasites, 'some of which are more minute,' he writes, 'than specks of dust.'

The university building where I work is shaped like a spaceship; there is something Star Trekky about its reverse flying buttresses that support its large upper half, its mangled shape built for far fewer rooms, and its elevators that run up and down what was once an outdoor courtyard. The married man sits three windowless rooms down from me. He sits near the door, and if it's cracked I can see him harnessed to his computer via headphones. If I go out, he often drops what he's doing and says, You going out? I'll go with you, takes off his earphones, and grabs his jacket.

We walk down the steel-lipped concrete stairs, cross the campus to the food trucks, and order tea. He orders green tea with coconut. I get Assam with a little cream. My hair's falling out, he says today, as soon as we're seated at one of the outdoor tables. I think I'm going to cut it short.

It's just barely warm enough to sit outside. We cup our hands around our teas. You'll look like your kids, I say.

I'll look like my father!

It's then that he begins to talk about the research he's doing. He's traced current school board politics to a series of racist emails, white superintendents let go with full retirement, benefits. He shakes his head. I guess, he admits, I'm a little depressed.

Don't tell me you're depressed, I say, because I'm really depressed. I don't have people here, except for you.

Same for me. You're my only friend here.

But you're married!

Yeah, I've thought about that. I don't want to break up my family. Is that even true? Yeah, it's true.

I don't want to do that, either, I hear myself say, my voice high and tinny.

As we part, I wonder how I am to make sense of such an afternoon at a place as seemingly inhuman as the one at which we've landed.

Months later, I fold the tinfoil wrapper of the burrito I am eating into a tiny, shiny, compact block, reducing it to something a crow might peck at. The married man takes off his glasses and lifts his shirt up to clean his lenses, thereby exposing his midline. I try not to let my eyes linger. I need to find a way to turn off my attraction and to love this man the only way possible: as a friend, as someone who revels in him calling me his people. I don't want to lose him, though part of me wonders whether the honest thing to do is to remove myself from the situation.

When the book of Horace Pippin's paintings arrives in the mail, I open it by chance to his *Woman Taken in Adultery*. I do not want to look at this painting and face the feelings I have for the married man. I do not want to see a representation of a woman being punished for something that is never just one person's doing. It is not until I read the Biblical story to which the painting's title alludes that I discover that, like in the other paintings Pippin painted that same year,[6] the point of view of the work actually sides with the underdog—in this case, the woman. [7]

---

[6] Pippin's 1941 paintings include *The Whipping*, in which a white master whips a slave tied to a post as another white man (pale as death) looks on, and *Christ Before Pilate*, in which a grey-colored Jesus, head bloodied by thorns, is condemned to death by a ghostly-white Pilate.
[7] Pippen's forgiving perspective of the figure of the adulteress might have unconsciously stemmed from his own questionable origins, as the woman Pippin called his mother was 53 when he was born. Pippin's actual mother was most likely the person he knew as his sister.

Romare Bearden saw Pippin's paintings as distortions away from photographic naturalism. Pippin, however, was adamant that his images were not distortions, but literal translations of the actual world. When I look at Pippin's paintings, especially his interiors in which there is usually a cook stove, kerosene lamps, throw rugs, and wooden tables, I am literally transported back to my childhood home my parents built: a stone house in the woods without electricity. Which reminds me: one day last fall, the married man pantomimed his younger self stacking brick while working with his mason father. Observing this act, I nearly keeled over, for I, too, had many a time searched for the right-shaped stone for whatever wall my pop was building.

Socrates' father was also a mason. I bring this up, because the other day the married man and I were talking about teaching and, out of the blue, he said that he felt like an imposter. I had just had a conversation with my father in which I had confessed suffering from exactly this same feeling. Look at my daughter, my father had said. My daughter, the professor!

So you think I'm too scruffy? I had asked. I was, at that moment, wearing ripped jeans and an old sweatshirt. Neither was Socrates a fancy dresser!

I just don't think anyone would believe you, if you told them what you do.

I feel like fraud myself, I'd said.

In Pippin's self-portrait (painted the same year he painted *Woman Taken in Adultery*), he gazes at a canvas on an easel, paintbrush in hand. The viewer can see nothing of what he is painting, only the edge of the canvas and some of its back. Yet the painting the viewer can't see is *this* self-portrait. We are actually looking at it.

Male gnats assemble in mating swarms called 'ghosts' around dusk. At the dog park, this evening, they are out in force. I swing my dog's leash above my head, trying to make it impossible for the little horse-driving boys to land. My dog, equally bothered, rubs her snout in the ground.

It is wrong of me to compare the 'divine truth' into which my dog and I are being driven by the *pusio* to the suffering of those who must contend with our mechanical reproductions of the insect world. So much has gone wrong. Where to begin to make anything right? I whistle for my dog. She hurries over and we leave the fenced-in compound. It is good to walk. There is a breeze, and I can almost imagine that I live somewhere near what hasn't yet been killed or trapped, what hasn't yet been studied for its stealth, what hasn't yet gone extinct. But just as I think we're out of the woods, my dog lies down, refusing to budge, and the little horse-driving boys zoom back.

An Era of Poppies

There was a basketball mural in the cafeteria, the restaurant in town served grits with runny eggs, and Yvonne taught me how to drive her pick-up truck down rural Alabama dirt roads. She was a woman on whose lap I gladly sat, window down, her feet at the pedals. Out in the field was the still my father built—a giant steel machine with blue breath that ate corn from the fields and transformed it into tractor gas. My tennis shoes had treads that made the earth's red dirt into Mickey Mouse heads, and I had a red horn on my bike that was a Christmas or birthday gift, and a *Ranger Rick* magazine that made me dream of animals, especially raccoons and deer and mink, and also of lobster crate races and snow sculptures. The winner of the lobster crate race was a girl with quick feet, who weighed little to nothing and seemed to fly over the water, barely sinking each crate. I wanted to be her, good at something. The children I played with didn't know what snow was. When I showed them my *Ranger Rick* magazine, they wanted to study the snow sculptures, whereas I wanted to look at the lobster crate race. There is a photograph of me with these children from that time and place in which I stand out as the one with white skin wearing a T-shirt that says, *I'm Me, Terrific, Adorable, Intelligent*, my hair parted by barrettes.

Candide's cheeks are perfectly round; her eyes glitter. She has the most infectious grin. She wears corn-rowed braids and an oversized T-shirt. Initially, Candide was a child of my imagination. I got her mixed up with my own self as a child. We were the same because we wore the same shirt. It was not the exact same shirt, but the one she wore in a photograph I saw of her was so similar to one I had worn at her age that I mixed us up. Her shirt read: *A Fully Fashionable Girl Comin' Downtown*. Last year, on my way to Kinshasa, Democratic Republic of the Congo, to visit Candide, I flew over Nigeria and looked down on the lush land where my parents met so many years ago and where my mother watched my father chase her lob across a clay tennis court and split open his head on a corner post. That evening no one was at the hospital. By the time a nurse appeared, my father's T-shirt was soaked with his own blood. The nurse searched for anesthesia. Unable to find any, she brought the lamp closer and sewed my father up without it.

When I was a child, whenever my parents and I returned home (after a day away, and after trudging through snow, our house still and dark in the distance), my mother would search in the dark for matches on the mantle and then sit at the dark table, taking the lamps' globes off, rolling up wicks and lighting them, and then carefully returning the globes to their mounts. The lamps seemed to swell as they turned blue. Sometimes the globes were smudged with soot. Mostly they were yellow where the flames licked them. It was my mother's job to light the lamps, my father's job to bring the wood in, stoke the stove, use the poker to move around any last dying piece of coal, and my job to crumple the newspaper up into balls. These were the firings of our house in the woods. This was coming home. It took some time for our presence to be made live, for our house to start breathing again. We clunked it back to life, we coaxed it. It groaned, sputtered, and sometimes it balked. We were cold. We needed it. It became itself a small fire. It opened itself to us gradually and glowed.

Candide, I said softly. I recognized her immediately. Her face was more ashen and she was smaller, somehow, than the photos had rendered her. Her braided hair was yellow-colored, a sign of malnutrition. She sat outside, near the orphanage office, in a plastic chair. She's upset, the orphanage director said, from something that happened at school.

What happened? I asked.

Fils spoke to Candide in Lingala. I heard Candide say something in a very quiet voice. She was yelled at, Fils translated.

An older woman came over and wiped Candide's nose with a hanky. Someone else brought me a chair. I sat down next to Candide and took out the pad I had brought for her and then began drawing her portrait. It was the only thing I knew to do. She was looking down, and I drew her this way using a blue colored pencil.

A few moments passed. Candide didn't move. When I finished, I held the page up to show her. She grinned. Then she bowed her head, squeezing tears out of her eyes, still smiling.

Man, that girl can smile, Fils said.

My father once called me out of the house to see a poppy bloom—its petals so delicate, like a tissue that had been balled. We watched the wrinkled red baby's fist unfurl in silence. It was early summer and the morning was not cool, not hot. My father was somewhat bent over; he did not yet use both walking sticks he later carved that now rest against the bookshelf. Each spring my father built trellises for his poppies wherever the previous year's seedpods had fallen. The trellises were vertical saplings he wired together, three feet high or so, tall enough to enclose and support the long poppy stalks that otherwise were rarely strong enough to uphold their own heavy heads and collapsed in high winds. One summer, my father drove me along Lakeshore Road to show me a field of poppies a neighbor had managed to grow. We later heard this man had first dumped a ton of pesticide in the soil. Before we knew this, we had wanted to sow flowers like that: a swath of color in a field.

After my father died, after his skin pulled taut over him, after he shrank, after his bones jutted out of his skin, after he was already gone before going, after I had to watch him unable to eat, unable to take a sip without choking, unable to cough without crying out, and after my mother had given him his liquid morphine, rubbing his cheek, his breath slowing (morphine, he told me, let him sleep in a straight line), the hospice nurse was called to the house. It was 4 a.m. The nurse had no sense that we—my mother who doesn't cry, and me who cries too much—did not want her bosomy hugs. Nor did we want the indignity of her ordering us, first thing, to get my father's morphine and some coffee grounds. Had we understood what was going on, we would have poured the drugs into the wood cook stove—it was on. Instead we retrieved for her the things she wanted: a plastic container, a plastic spoon, the coffee grounds, and then sat with her at our walnut table, the one my father crafted, while she stirred the white pills and clear liquid into the plastic container full of still-hot grounds. After she finished stirring, she broke the plastic spoon in half, wincing, and added the broken spoon to the mixture. As I duct taped the container shut as per her instructions, I thought of the people who had worked so hard to supply us with those drugs, people who had moved their families to the fields, built huts near the poppies, scored the ovaries of the flower pods two weeks after the petals dropped, and then collected the cuts' drips; people who knew the delicate flower's crown had to tilt skyward before they could score it—and only then come late afternoon, so that the white latex would flow without drying too quickly in the sun and clogging the cut. These farmers know that opium darkens and thickens on cool nights, like the blood did on my father's gums. An hour before he died, his gums turned black, and while my mother stoked the woodstove, I moistened his thin lips with lemon water.

Candide lined the things I brought for her up in her lap. Yoyo, Candide's best friend, tied the gaping hole in the plastic bag up in a knot. Candide then put her pad and colored pencils in it. Madness is a type of living, a vulnerable band that, when stretched too far, refuses to retract—refuses its labor; a mirror reflecting the mark of society's gaze, rendering a woman unwhole who is without child. The power of a photograph, of a series of phone calls, of entertaining and then believing oneself to be a mother and then not becoming one is none other than a miscarriage. Yet Candide is alive. I once chose her from among all the orphans of the world to mother, back before anyone knew she carries the virus that killed all three of her siblings and her parents. She smiled at me during dinner in a way a child had never before smiled at me. I smiled back. The sun got more brilliant. And then night fell. Candles were lit along roadside stands and men rode on the tailgates of trucks. Single parent adoptions have since closed in the DRC and I've had to leave Candide where she is.

Now it is so hot in Phoenixville, Pennsylvania, that the watercress leaves point downward. The family living on the porch below, young parents and their two-year-old, use the downstairs washer. The smell of their laundry soap invades my apartment. There is something about what happens in heat that magnifies bewilderment. I place notes on the washing machine after buying natural soap, begging them to use it. But the young mother tells me she won't wash her clothes in that.

Whatever, I say, as I exit the porch.

She says, We'll only be here a week. She has said this since the beginning of the summer. If you're going to have an attitude about it, she adds.

I cry on the way to the grocery store because I have wanted one thing and one thing only, a child, for so long now and have worked so hard to adopt that the rest of my life has shriveled.

In a stuccoed, low-ceilinged room, Candide gets ready for school. She buttons her white blouse and ties her shoelaces into a series of crocheted knots. She is ten years old and thin as a stalk of sorghum. I have lived with her light and shadow for years. She is my other half. Soon she will walk up a dusty road along which women in dirt courtyards wash their clothes and sheets, sort grain, and scrub dishes in plastic tubs. The wind this morning stirs the palm fronds. A man pulls a dug-out from the Congo River. Mammoth logs swallow the river's sandy shore as cranes lift them into train cars.

I can't sleep. I am remembering my father on a lobster boat in Greece. It's my birthday. I'm ten. I'm in the sand by Fofo's guesthouse near the baby chicks. I'm wearing my green corduroy overalls with the straps that cross in back. My hair is the length it is now—shoulder-length, brown. My skin is brown from the sun. I walk across the beach. There is seaweed everywhere. I've cut my heel. We can't ride our bikes. I am strong enough for hundred-mile days, but I'm happy I'm hurt. I want to stay here with Fofo and the chicks. At a tavern in town, my parents gift me a goat bell. It is my heart. It is the perfect gift, the perfect object. I will never love anything as much. My father writes me a poem and draws little pictures around it. I am his flat-footed, goat-eyed girl. I want to be his flat-footed, goat-eyed girl forever.

I keep my father's copy of *Immortal Poems* by the window. I chose it, of all his possessions, and the hoodie I gave him that he never wore, but that I dressed him in the day before he died. Some days I zip myself in. Some days I'm him.

He comes to me as I cut bread. I see him at the stone counter in Essex, New York, folding dough out on the counter, flour everywhere. I see his expression; he's concentrating on the bread, doing things quickly. He has it down. He has his bread towel. He has his bowl. He has his French Oven. He would almost seem angry pounding that bread. On the floor by my bed: a stone-headed bird with a wire body—a sculpture my father made me. I look at its fossil eye, its twisted wire and gold-soldered body. In it, I can see my father's quickness of touch, the way he always went after everything physically.

I eat coconut cake and drink a black tea, remembering the cremation smoke in Kathmandu and the trickle of a river. Long ago, I crossed that river. I remember bicycling through the human smoke. It felt right. Death was part of life. There was a real feeling that to pass through that smoke was to make a journey from one place to another. At the top of the hill was the monkey temple. The monkeys had taken it over as their swinging gym. The city on the other side of the river was filled with grit, people, the chaos of cars. But on this side of the river, there were rats, monkeys, girls with dolls. It was such a shock to be seventeen in that place, the lepers without fingers, legs, noses, begging on the streets on their handmade skateboards; the pregnant leper who attached herself to me. A deep depression followed. I recall writing in my notebook one morning at the fish market in New York City, about how death was largely hidden in this nation, how I had forgotten my childhood in the forest and been separated from everything that had ever meant something to me and been forced out into the world. I wrote this, even though I had been rearing to go, had left home at fifteen, not looked back, been too eager.

Airports are shutting down in Guinea, Sierra Leone, Nigeria. Sick persons arrive in Atlanta, Madrid, New Mexico. Soon we will all wear suits. It will be unsafe to engage in sex. We will die out in mad dashes. These are my thoughts before I censor them. Before the traffic erases them. Before the dog must be walked, and, so, the everyday becomes the norm. It is the abiding fact that love exists, but that there is nobody near. I was alive once. There were tastes of the inevitable, and there were tastes that were extreme. There was the thought that I would find love. And there was the idea that perhaps there was a meeting place between spirits, a mountain ledge at which souls exchanged some kind of beating. Then they stood up, bowed, and repeated the disturbance. Now there is no such knowledge.

There are cross-wirings. The way a computer can drop a signal. The way a man can come, test for something, find nothing wrong, but there still be a problem. This is the code word for lost. Outside, beyond these crumbling walls, people die. Then there are desk killers, like me, who know what is happening, who protest inside their souls, loving in secret. I think of those days I spoke to someone of my mother who never felt herself loved enough. Was I speaking of realizing myself, of choosing this over love—or over not-great-enough love? If I didn't speak exactly of this, this is what I meant. Perhaps I thought that the person sitting across from me could understand, but why did I think this?

Tears come knowing how close we are and how far apart we must remain. Mostly, I think of my father. Then I think of a girl half a world away. Feel things, someone says. When you feel things, problems resolve on their own.

I don't believe this. Instead, I believe that wars will come ever closer, invading this country like a virus.

This evening there is another domestic dispute outside. I do not know that I can take another. Years of living beside such violence. Years of stomaching my own brokenness. Now, when a man screams, I hope you fucking die, I know that no one should wish this upon any other.

All I see is my father's bloody mouth, his stiffened body being carried away in the rain.

In the winter, igloos used to grow attached to the outside of our house. My father and I shoveled, packed, and shaped the blocks of snow-ice, piling them up against the thick wall of stone. This was the wall I kicked my soccer ball against. I knew the stones, their yellow-pink-grey hues, how they fit together. We let the igloos melt there; we let them wet the stone. While they lasted, we sat inside them, blissful, insolated. The igloos rested, propped up against the house, flying buttresses, loose teeth, things that couldn't stand not to be attached, spaces made just for me. I basked in them and hated their impermanence. Our house itself was a stone monument I knew how to climb. A roof whose shingle I'd touched. The wood on the backside of the house turned grey in time with rot from snow and rain.

The ceiling stained. Sometimes the house smoked. Sometimes it showed me mink through its pane glass windows. Mostly it felt like old clothes in cold closets and sounded like stories I buried my nose in. Once in a while we listened to something fine on the radio. There was time. Things were in harmony back then when my mother and father were all that I wanted.

Candide in a peach-colored dress. I've never seen anyone so beautiful, never loved anyone so much. This is what it means to mother—to stand guard at the very handrails of what can't be guarded. Trapped by circumstance, I try to crawl on my belly past the barricade. My body becomes leaner, meaner, and I become more silent.

My father as he approached death was thin and unbearably sweet-natured. There was also the confusion and drug-altered questions and fears. He would hold onto my arm and say, Get me out of here. Or he would ask, in a horrible voice, When?

He'd basically lost his voice by the end, and so the hoarseness, the hurt of his throat, all of it meant he was suffering. Many of us are deluded enough, or perhaps hopeful enough, to think that there is something better, always, around the corner, no matter which corner. My father wasn't one of these people. Maybe a month before he died, he said that this wasn't the life he had expected.

As I age, it seems, the less I am able to believe in the narratives we throw around as the expected ones. They don't seem possible, probable, or even worthy. To be able to visit in the mind of another, in the body of another, to be given a piece of a person's soul and commune with it—this is life and art.

My father's body is now in a cardboard box. His ashes, my mother says, are heavy.

This morning I stopped to see the poppies. One was popping. The flower still had its hairy cap perched atop its blood red curled up, crepe-paper-like heart. I sat down in front of it and waited. The red of the flower pulsed. Behind it other poppies swayed. To the left were dried poppy heads filled with black seeds the size of grains of sand. The poppy's cap separated from its stalk. I stuck out a hand. I wanted to catch the cap as the petals pushed it off, but the cap hung on. A female grosbeak came to water from the rain-filled cavity in the stone beside me. Purple Russian sage colored the interior of the garden. Stone birds my father sculpted stood stock still. A fly alighted on my palm. Then a sweat bee joined it, its double-yellow striped abdomen busily waving. Lastly, a midge stopped for a brief second. I kept my palm out. The unfolding happened ever-so-slowly. My eyes focused and unfocused. The force of the opening petals thrust the cap up ever higher. I was still poised to catch it. But when the tiny, green, hairy cap fell, it tumbled out of my hand and into the grass.

Once upon a time, my father called me out to watch a poppy open.

A Short History of Hostile Soil

On The Barrens

I am on hostile soil. That's what the sign posted at the tree line skirting the Unionville Serpentine Barrens, in Chester County, Pennsylvania, says. The Barrens—a total of seven acres at the edge of a thousand-plus acre preserve—is home to serpentine, a green rock that rose out of cracks in the Iapetus Ocean floor a half-billion years ago. Serpentine, in which jade is often found, is also laced with asbestos and its high mineral content leeches into adjacent soil, rendering such earth inhospitable and toxic for most plant life. Plants in such infertile soil frequently rot to death. Certain plant species, however, have adapted to the high concentrations of magnesium, nickel, cobalt, chromium, and iron, and low concentrations of calcium, nitrogen, and phosphorus, not to mention the drought-like conditions and high soil temperatures that result from the unusually water-absorbent clays (formed from minerals) and from lack of shade cast by little blue stem, Indian-grass, and side oats gramma grasses. Some trees live here too—the blackjack oak, post oak, pitch and Virginia pines, and eastern red cedar, but they are stunted and offer little cover. Although this spot is called The Barrens, serpentinization is thought to have aided the emergence of life on earth, given that geothermically heated hydrogen released during the green rock's formation combined with carbon dioxide to form organic compounds, including hydrocarbons and fatty acids—key energy sources for metabolism. What does it mean to stand here? I square myself to the elements and bow my head into the wind.

On property

Long before Nietzsche pronounced that God was dead, Karl Marx acknowledged '*geognosy*—i.e., from the science, which presents the formation of the earth, the development of the earth, as a process, as a self-generation' and disregarded the question of any higher power. Such a question was abstract, whereas 'the *real existence* of man and nature' was evident, Marx argued, 'through sense experience.' It was such sense experience that led Marx to his concept of the *human being*. An individual's ability to see, hear, smell, taste, feel, think, observe, experience, want, act, and love were social in essence, Marx posited. The abolition of private property is therefore, he wrote in 1866, 'the complete *emancipation* of all human senses and qualities.' Possessing land or nature—or a woman—was, Marx believed, *the* gateway drug to use and abuse. Private property depended upon the labor of others, and its formation bespoke the self-estrangement of the capitalist laborer. *Human sense*, however, Marx argued, regarded nature in its entirety—no alienation about it. And, as man's relation to woman was equivalent to his relation to nature, a man's need was a *human* need. Therefore, man's need for 'an *other* person as a person' exemplified that his individual existence was also a social existence. The annulment of private property, for Marx, was the recognition of the vileness of ownership and signified a return of man to himself. Communism, Marx predicted, would transform all property into the hands of the commons and require everyone to work for the benefit of the community. It wouldn't last, but it was, he thought, the next step in man's essential development.

Regardless whether one argues that Communist lands are most corrupt and polluted today, I continue to turn to Marx, admiring him as a thinker who somehow understood that man's obsession with ownership was killing not only the human, it was killing all life. I bring all this up, because I first visited The Barrens with a man named Ter who once quarried and set stone with my father.

We didn't speak of my father, the day Ter and I walked across the ancient grassland, but my father's essence seemed to hover in the air above the soil, and I remember picking up several feathers almost perfectly camouflaged by snow-speckled Indian-grass. When my father died, half of the quarry, which he owned together with Ter, fell into my mother's hands. My mother and I verbally agreed that Ter would become the quarry's sole owner (something I felt was only right, given the amount Ter and his family had done for our family throughout my father's long illness). But several months later my mother, seeming to have forgotten altogether that she and I had had this discussion, mentioned selling the quarry, in passing, to me.

I emailed Ter, alarmed. Did you know, I asked him, that my mother is speaking of selling the quarry?

Ter emailed back to say that he hadn't known. But, he said, he knew that there were a few interested buyers, including a man whose brother had originally wanted to make the quarry into a gravel business. My father and Ter had talked for years about securing the quarry for future public access.

Despite my love for my mother, I placed myself squarely between her and Ter, making it known that I would mediate, if need be, so as to protect the land my father had cared for, quarrying only what he easily could, not blasting for rock, but splitting the seams of fossil-rich, cloud-grey limestone by plug and feather.

On The Barrens again: an email from Ter

Conservationists are wanting to preserve that natural grassland community of plants and animals...but now have to perform regular managed burns to discourage invasives which weren't around until more recent times. They also appear to be haying the fields (after nesting birds fledge)... Does the natural community withstand the haying? I guess...but that doesn't seem like a natural process to me. Anyway, it was a beautiful place to stroll about.

On invasives

My mother is, at this minute, out in the field in front of her house, cutting the flower heads off the poison parsnip—an invasive that can burn a person's skin. The plant looks like Queen Anne's lace (also an invasive), but its flowers are yellow and more spread out, rather than centered in one large crown. It is reported to be 'most tenacious,' 'aggressive,' and 'venomous,' and to readily move into 'disturbed habitats.' After slowly building up an initial population, wild parsnip spreads rapidly, according to various websites, its prolific reproductive capacities changing soil chemistry and causing genetic changes in native plant relatives through hybridization, and sometimes spreading harmful plant pathogens. As I read about how the parsnip once 'jumped the fences of colonial gardens' and about its 'belligerent ability' to 'push out native plants,' poised as it is to cause economic (supposedly billions of dollars of damage annually), environmental, and human harm, I am not surprised by the webpage's accompanying ad—a photograph of people standing with their hands over their chests together with a caption that reads: 'TEST YOUR KNOWLEDGE: Could you pass a U.S. citizenship test?'

I take the citizenship test and score a 76%. I'm marginally a citizen. (I score an 81% on the African geography quiz.) I imagine my lack of patriotism has something to do with the fact that I grew up thinking that the invasive chicory, when it flowered, was the best color on the planet. I still think it is. Perhaps the wild yellow parsnip and the blue chicory will hybridize and soon we'll be drinking a green-colored Starbucks Frapchicnips. But will this, in any way, impact the ongoing war against the wild parsnip?

On world citizenship
The World Government for World Citizens—a 'political representation of the sovereign citizen of the world dynamically, intrinsically allied with sovereign humanity'—was founded by Garry Davis, a WWII bomber, who renounced (though he argued there was nothing to renounce given that national citizenship was an 18th century fiction rendered obsolete by technological revolutions) his U.S. citizenship in protest of his own wartime actions. He had flown bombing missions over Brandenburg, in part to avenge the death of his brother who had died in the Allied invasion of Italy, but it hadn't helped. Davis couldn't forget that his bombs had killed civilians.

To be a global citizen, according to Davis, one recognizes his or her rights and duties within the world community, including 'essential kinship with nature and all other species sharing life on this world.' A world citizen must still pay national taxes for whatever is deemed peaceful. One does not, however, and this is Davis's winning point, have to pay war taxes. Rather, one pays the amount equivalent to the war tax to the World Government for World Citizens, and then attaches a form letter (provided by Davis) to one's partial tax return that states that one is 'sanctioned by Article 28, Universal Declaration of Human Rights, (inter alia),' and that one is acting 'in accordance with Article 15(2) of the aforementioned Declaration (inter alia)' and with respect to one's 'world civic rights and duties as defined in part by the aforementioned Declaration, and in conformity with international law as defined by the Nuremberg Principles (inter alia).'

Before Davis died (in the Vermont town where I was reared), he granted a world passport to the stranded Edward Snowden whose U.S. passport had been revoked by U.S. authorities. (Snowden was then and is still wanted by the U.S. for leaking details of state surveillance programs.) Two days later, however, Snowden was still holed up in the Moscow airport, as Ecuador had refused to accept his world passport. Most of Snowden's other requests for asylum were rejected on the condition that he needed to be present on whatever respective country's soil to submit his application. Regardless, Snowden eventually received several asylum offers. Travelling to any one of those countries would not have required a passport under the United Nation's 1951 Refugee Convention, so Davis's issuing Snowden a world passport was largely a symbolic gesture, and, as it turned out, Snowden accepted Russian asylum and no international travel was necessary.

I am not a passport or card-carrying, non-war-tax-paying World Citizen. (My parents, though, once received a letter threatening government seizure of their house and property for refusing to pay their war tax during the war in Vietnam.) Still, I think a lot about war taxes and who I've paid to have killed in my name, just as I often pause to consider what ground I've personally polluted, what traces of depleted uranium are associated with my income. But I would have to agree with the human rights organizations that criticize Davis's world citizen passport for offering refugees false hope for the $45 such a passport costs, just as I suspect my carrying a world passport would mire me in a mountain of paperwork and would most likely totally disable my current attempt to internationally adopt a child. It's true that the world passport is important as a political symbol of the fiction of borders, but this fiction, like the fiction of race, remains nonetheless incredibly real today. Witness the consequences of being a non-citizen and/or someone raced in this fascist age.

On the importance of soil
For some time in early North America, only white male landowners were citizens and could vote. As my mother puts it, You had to own the soil, not just be born on it to vote, and because women and slaves didn't own soil, they couldn't vote; they were chattel.

What is chattel? I ask. I mean, I know the word, but where does it come from?

I don't know, my mother says.

I look it up. Chattel is, the dictionary states, an item of property other than real estate, and derives from the Middle English 'cattle.' We were cattle, I tell her.

Now I want to know what happens to those who aren't born on actual soil. I look this up, too. It turns out that the U.S. adheres to the 1961 Convention on Reduction of Statelessness which contests that if parents are citizens of the country of registration of the aircraft or ship on which a child is born that this nationality is also the child's. Other nations adhere to other conventions. As for those who are born on soil but whose soil disappears (for instance, citizens of island nations who may soon become environmental migrants' displaced by climate change), such persons are or will be forced outside the traditional statehood criteria, according to international law. In other words, a citizen is a resident of a particular land. (And isn't even a world citizen beholden to worldly geography?)

On statehood
Indian journalist R. Jagannathan finds statehood based on territory an archaic western concept. Take ISIS, for example. 'Regardless of whether or not all Muslim countries coalesce as one political entity and accept the ISIS chief Abu Bakr al-Baghdadi as Caliph (fat chance!),' Jagannathan writes, 'the intent clearly follows the western ideal of what a nation is—a group of people united by common ideals and a common past interested in creating a common future jointly.' Europe's definition of nation as people of a similar ethnicity confined within a geography has dominated the world for the past 400 years, Jagannathan reminds us. The refinement of the notion of the nation by Ernest Renan, a 19th century French historian, as a territory of people with 'common glories in the past' and 'common will in the present' and who perform 'great deeds together' and 'wish to perform more' was realized, Jagannathan adds, by Hitler. Every despot, he insists, dreams this same dream. ISIS has established footholds worldwide with its $3 billion network facilitated by military campaigning, Internet, and media presence.

What's intriguing about Jagannathan's critique is that he doesn't stop with ISIS's hunger for statehood. He critiques western governments for revoking the citizenship of those who join ISIS. While arguing against statehood as a dated concept, Jagannathan nonetheless is forced to acknowledge the fundamental right of nationality. Statelessness often renders people vulnerable to human rights violations, just as anti-terror laws that strip citizenship from terrorist suspects remove government and constitutional accountability. Such individuals make for easy targets, and are often tortured, detained indefinitely, and killed.

On stealing the self

Before the abolition of slavery in the U.S., a slave was considered a piece of property, which meant, Angela Davis writes, that when a slave 'escaped from slavery, he also stole property which belonged, in the eyes of the law, to his master.' A fugitive slave was considered by state and federal law to be a criminal, 'a thief who absconded with his own body,' Davis adds. Post-abolition, the erasure and disappearing of the citizen was extended to those imprisoned by the convict lease system and thereafter by the prison-industrial complex which today still denies those imprisoned the right to vote. Targets of U.S. military drone strikes also have little recourse other than to abscond with their own bodies.

To compare the erasure of the citizen of the slave era to the erasure of the citizen today, let us examine two famous legal cases—the first, the 1857 case of slave Dred Scott's attempt to become a U.S. citizen and, the second, a case put forward in 2011 by Anwar al-Awlaki's father after learning that his son, a U.S. citizen, had been placed on the U.S. government's kill list. In the first case, Scott sued for his and his family's freedom, arguing that, because his family had lived with their master in a number of states and territories where slavery was illegal, their master had forfeited his legal right to hold them in bondage. The case, however, was decided against Scott when Chief Justice Roger B. Taney ruled that no person of African descent, whether a slave or not, could be a citizen of the U.S. and that therefore Scott had no legal standing to file a suit in federal court. Similarly, in al-Awlaki's case, the Justice Department invoked the state-secrets privilege and the lawsuit was thereby dismissed by the district court with Judge John Bates who stated that this political question could only be decided by the president and ruled that al-Awlaki's father had no legal standing to file a suit on his son's behalf; he could only file after his son was killed. After the case was decided, Anwar al-Awlaki was indeed killed by drone strike together with another American citizen, Samir Khan, in Yemen. Not only were these two men murdered in plain sight and by a government that had excused itself of any accountability, but two weeks following this attack, An-war's sixteen-year-old son, Rahman, also an American citizen, was killed by drone strike while collecting his father's body for burial. Neither Anwar al-Awlaki nor his son had ever had any charges brought against them. And, in fact, killing of U.S. citizens had, until this time, been prohibited by the Constitution's due process clause. But the Justice Department's Office of Legal Counsel thereafter prepared a secret legal memo, asserting that while the Fifth Amendment's guarantee of due process applied, it could only be satisfied by the president's deliberations. In other words, whosoever the president decided to kill, and for whatever reason he deemed necessary, the president's word was law.

Legal ratification to justify drone strikes began with Bill Clinton, and was ratcheted up by George W. Bush who set it more firmly into place three days after 9/11, after Congress gave him permission to use necessary and appropriate force against those he determined had aided the attacks or who harbored said persons or groups, providing the president with plausible deniability for secret intelligence killings. Following the killing of Samir Khan, Anwar al-Awlaki, and al-Awlaki's son Rahman, President Obama further nullified *habeas corpus* (a person's right to challenge in court the legality of his or her imprisonment), extending it over foreign nationals *and* U.S. citizens. Authorized at this time, as well, was indefinite detention without trial or indictment of any U.S. citizen designated an enemy by the president.

Legal authorities can no longer exercise control over President Obama's power. Justice Department's Office of Legal Counsel John Yoo's Unitary Executive theory has additionally put an end to the principles of the separation of powers as defined by Montesquieu. Not unlike The Barrens' serpentinite rock that jumpstarted all life *and* also creates toxic living conditions, such a state of exception enables the president to protect life *and* authorize holocausts. In effect, it gives him legal power to suspend the validity of the law. He alone makes the final decision between membership and inclusion, between what is outside and what is inside, between exception and rule, and, thus, he decides, as Giorgio Agamben would have it, which life may be killed without the commission of homicide. The problem of a sovereign power, like President Obama's, as Agamben argues, is that it renders modern democracy constitutionally incapable of imagining a politics as separate from the state and makes all citizens into *homines sacri* (what Pompeius Festus called sacred men—those persons whose murders would not be punished).

And because the state of exception also allows a president to protect life, it was, somewhat coincidentally, just such a suspension of law that once helped usher in the end of slavery. In 1860, Lincoln—who had previously addressed a crowd with the words, 'We desired the court to have held that they [Dred Scott, his wife, and two daughters] were citizens so far at least as to entitle them to a hearing as to whether they were free or not; and then, also, that they were in fact and in law really free'—was elected president. A year later, fearing that federal troops would be stopped by rebels from marching through Maryland, Lincoln suspended *habeas corpus* along the Philadelphia to Washington railroad line, arguing that this suspension was essential to preserving the Union. And after issuing this state of exception and acting as an absolute dictator for two years, Lincoln issued the Emancipation Proclamation, which, before slavery was abolished outright, had to be followed by the ratification of the Thirteenth Amendment which, in 1865, came to read: 'Neither slavery nor involuntary servitude, except as a punishment for crime whereof the party shall have been duly convicted, shall exist within the United States, or any place subject to their jurisdiction'—with, of course, the wording 'except as a punishment' opening up a legal loophole for the continued abuse of freed slaves, as rarely was any freed slave 'duly convicted.' In any event, an era that had opened with the troubling Dred Scott Decision had spiraled into a war that had ended with the securing of citizenship for African Americans.

In contrast, the killing of al-Awlaki and his son has garnered little public outrage. Comparing and contrasting Lincoln's and Obama's suspension of *habeas corpus* and their uses of the state of exception, it's obvious that Lincoln drew upon the force of law to mobilize troops to protect the State and thereby justly to expand citizen rights, whereas Obama continues to draw upon the force of law to protect the State at the unjust expense of citizens'—and others'—rights.

If racism generalizes the right to kill anyone, drone strikes have generalized the president's right to kill Muslim persons. In fact, Akbar Ahmed accuses the U.S. of targeting tribal Islam ('some of the most impoverished and isolated [communities] in the world') simply for being tribal

Islamists rather than for being suspects of any particular crime. Two of Pakistan's newspapers have calculated the vast majority of drone strikes in Pakistan (where a majority of drone strikes have taken place since Obama identified the Northwest region of the country as the preeminent hotbed for the breeding of extremist elements) kill civilian tribesmen. Tribesmen, already suffering from impoverishment, are vanishing, Ahmed claims. As Qadir Khan, a Pakistani tribesman, confesses, 'Life of a tribesman is so valueless that anyone who wants to bleed a human can come and fire at a tribesman and no question will be asked.'

Such drone attacks, not only fit the definition of genocide, they serve to foment blowback, precisely because Tribal Islamists in South Waziristan adhere to 'code of the Pukhtun, generally referred to as Pukhtunwali,' which 'is a combination of hospitality, revenge, and the constant compulsion to safeguard what is normatively understood as honor,' as Ahmed explains. Blowback finds its most potent weapon in the suicide bomb, as tribesmen have no weapons, means, or method to counter the drone; all they have are their bodies. Not unlike slaves in the U.S. who once turned to suicide as a preference over continued servitude, tribesmen (suffering from the psychological impact of 'the constant threat of random annihilation' by drone strike) choose, in seeking to substantiate their tribal honor, to annihilate themselves.

On the wanted unwanted

It is the summer that isn't, as my mother said today. It is the summer of incessant rain and wicked winds, the summer David Sweat is shot twice in the torso while running across a field. He has pop-tarts in his bag and has sprinkled pepper on his trail. Within just two miles of the Canadian border, he is shot in Constable, New York. The police in the photos on Google are pictured wearing plastic gloves—not unlike the ones worn in the Abu Ghraib photos—and holding up Sweat's bare, bleeding torso. Why would you jog through a town with such a name if you were an escaped convict? I ask my mom.

We are inside, watching it rain. The windows are closed, but we are no longer scared to open them. Had we really been scared? We'd laughed at the news that two felons might be knocking at our door in the middle of the night, even though someone had spotted them—or two men who looked like them—just a mile from my mom's. Police had swarmed thicker than blackflies. Armed neighbors patrolled every outbuilding up and down the road. And despite our good humor, there were times my mother and I had spooked ourselves, times when hearing a noise in a shed had given us pause and when shots in a field garnered suspicions of something other than some farmer aiming at a sick animal or doe out of season. We'd followed Sweat's story; it was impossible not to. It was all anyone had talked about.

I tell my mother now that I would have made wings and climbed a tree or fire tower—done something outlandish—tried to fly, had I been the one on the run. It occurs to me as I say this that Sweat was caught in the town where I, at age seven, learned how to jump out of a plane—or at least where I once practiced the moves of how to skydive while jumping from a wooden platform together with a kid who now BASE jumps in a wing suit.

Storms have wiped out my mom's spinach, quinoa, peas, and my gourds are yellowing in wet soil. Nothing is growing. The TV's on, even though my mom and I are more focused on the rain—the climate has become more severe. We're told it will rain more here over the next however many years. We'll have to change what we plant. The rain doesn't abate. In the wet wind, the basswoods leaves lash the top of the house (the roof boasting sheets of bright, almost fluorescent green moss). In the background, the newscaster is saying for the tenth time, 'Blood, he's coughing up blood.'

Who is this 35-year-old Sweat, imprisoned at 17, who never again lived for any length of time as a free man? Who can he be, jogging off across a field and letting a cop take a shot—two shots—at him? Does he still think Joyce is in love with him? 'Giggled like a schoolgirl around him,' an ex-convict told a British tabloid. 'It was like the high school jock asking out the ugly girl,' he added.

Joyce's husband still believes Joyce loves him. He says she swore on her son's head that she never slept with Sweat. But it increasingly seems that maybe she'd been planning all along to kill her husband and run off to Mexico with Sweat and Matt—the other convict she helped escape and offered other favors to. Sweat and Matt cut their way out of their cell and through sewer pipes with tools Joyce smuggled in for them in frozen meat. A reporter now jogs through a Malone neighborhood to get to Alice Hyde Medical Center to report on Sweat's critical condition. Matt is dead. The

186

cops shot him three times in the head the day I ran over a chipmunk with my car and had to watch it run in tortured circles afterward. I'd felt so badly, refused to speak, driven guiltily on. I should have stopped the car, done something, I'd said.

Another car will, mom had replied.

Men being hunted in the woods—it had thrown me. I'd thought of runaway slaves, the underground railroad stop just down the road, and John Brown's farm up the way. And what are my mom and I talking about? I'm talking about flying. I have the audacity to imagine building wings and climbing a tree. It's still unbelievable to me that we can find escaped convicts, my mother is saying.

We live, I say, in a surveillance state.

This has been a particularly harrowing year with a massive amount of publicized (thanks to recording devices) killings of blacks by cops, and here is Sweat, a white cop killer (Sweat did not just repeatedly shoot a cop, he ran the cop who was still conscious over with his car) shot twice for capture, which really means: shot twice for the story of how exactly such an escape from a maximum security prison happened.

Let me go home, I sob as I drive through the storm until I can't drive anymore. It's a day after Sweat's capture. I've had to leave my mom and drive back to a state where I wish I didn't live—home of 'hostile soil.' I pull over at a gas station. One of the gas pumps has just been struck by lightning and the dinging inside the station won't stop. I have to keep working the register for another three hours, the girl behind the counter says.

The sky looks black. A guy comes over to the coffee (I'm pouring myself one) and asks which direction I'm headed, cause he knows it can't be south. Cars are all over the road in water this deep—I work for a tow company, he says.

I have bad luck, I tell my mom over the phone.

You just lived through the escaped convicts! she says.

Yeah, I tell the girl at the counter, as I pay for my coffee, my mom still on the line. My mom lives in upstate New York and you know some convicts—

The girl nods.

I've basically been under house arrest and now this—

The girl and I look outside and shake our heads.

On the top Google hits

Googling 'hostile soil' introduces me to Vic Hummert (reared 'in a small Illinois town where there has been only one murder in 150 years') who cites Thoreau's quip, 'Why build a house if we do not have a friendly Earth upon which to put it,' and blogs about the melting of glaciers and acidification of the ocean. I'm led, as well, to a sci-fi website that boasts the following quote from Frank Herbert's *Dune* (dubbed by some 'the first planetary ecology novel on a grand scale'): 'How easy it is to kill the uprooted plant, especially when you put it down in hostile soil.' I discover, too, that in the Philippines development of 'a promising plant microorganism,' commercially known as the Hi-Q Vam, is being injected into tree roots to 'help trees survive hostile soil conditions'—the result of decades of unsustainable farming, grazing, and ore extraction. A report from Australia also suggests that adding large quantities of poultry manure to dense clay sub-soils can return profits to farms with hostile soil within a few years. Although the cost of mixing manure slurry deep into sub-soil is high, the article furthers, pressure to produce more food is rising as the island's population grows and land is consumed by urban sprawl.

Google also turns up James Kent's pontifications on the legal ramifications as per who owns the produce of hostile soil during wartime. Kent, once Chancellor of the State of New York and a Professor of Law at Columbia University, had a soft spot it seems for justice across the color line. He not only opposed raising the property qualifications for black voters, he argued that blacks and slaves, born in the United States, were 'natural born subjects,' just as whites were subjects 'bound by allegiance and subjection to the government and law of the land.' In 1866, the year that Congress, at long last, conceded that all persons born on U.S. soil were entitled to citizenship, Kent wrote in his Commentary on International Law that 'produce of a hostile soil bears a hostile character,' and that

> whoever owns or possesses land in the enemy's country, though he may in fact reside elsewhere, and be in every other respect a neutral or friend, must be taken to have incorporated himself with the nation, so far as he is a holder of the soil, and the produce of that soil is held to be enemy's property, independent of the personal residence or occupation of the owner.

In other words, Kent is saying here that the produce of hostile soil is rife for the taking, but he's also stating that hostility is linked to soil, and that, regardless from where one hails, soil is *the* binding clause.

On my constitution

Perhaps it is the fusion of nation with soil and the implied understanding of an enemy as one who lives upon 'hostile soil' that has me as if spell-bound by The Barrens. I've always rooted for the underdog. And, if I feel like I am living on hostile soil these days, it is not just because the war on terror has affected my conception of what hostile soil actually is, what with international private militias, secret black sites around the world, and no true way to gauge who is or is not a terrorist; it is because I no longer feel at home anywhere. Even being a world citizen would do little to help me escape the madness of civilization. Drones, gunmen, escaped convicts, and environmental catastrophe do not heed national borders. My parents once subscribed to the 'far out isn't far enough' back-to-the-land movement. I was reared without electricity in the woods. Today, however, my genera-tion isn't attempting to revel in nature; those of us who care are attempting to save its remnants, archiving seeds and freezing the eggs and sperm of mammals that are going extinct faster than we can harvest their unborn. Alan Weisman in *The World Without Us*, however, is hopeful: without us, life will continue. We invasives, we serpentine creatures, we haters of our own species, we owners of everything can only be so destructive. Our de-mise promises new life.

On coincidence

Last night I awoke in the middle of the night. I drank watermelon juice and, unable to fall back to sleep, pulled out a paperback I had been read-ing—Primo Levi's *The Periodic Table*. I read along, engaged by the beauty of the language, as Levi is, aside from being a concentration camp survivor, an incredible storyteller, until I came to the word 'serpentine.' I started. I back-pedaled, rereading several of the pages I had just read, so as to fully understand why it was that I was—in the middle of my own exploration of serpentine—now coming across Levi's. Of course! The chapter I was read-ing was titled 'Nickel.' Levi had been drafted, after finishing his studies, to work as a chemist in a secret mine. In this mine, there was asbestos everywhere. Ashy snow, Levi called it. The Italian army wanted to enrich the 0.2 percent of nickel found in the serpentine rock. Such was Levi's task, shadowy as it was, in the face of the looming threat to his Jewish existence. At his most weary, Levi perceived the rock that encircled him, 'the green serpentine of the Alpine foothills, in all its sidereal, hostile, extraneous hardness,' as rock he had to wrestle like a 'white whale,' as, he wrote, 'one should not surrender to incomprehensible matter, one must not just sit down. We are here for this—'

And so Levi heated the serpentine to 800 degrees Centigrade and then, as it cooled, passed hydrogen through it, reversing its creation. Thereafter he sat with a magnet and for hours in the early morning picked apart filigrees of 6 percent nickel and 94 percent wispy iron from the otherwise green-turned-yellow mass of serpentine. 'I was not thinking,' he wrote, 'that if the method of extraction I had caught sight of could have found industrial application, the nickel produced would have entirely ended up in Fascist Italy's and Hitler Germany's armor plate and artillery shells,' nor was he, it turned out, thinking that he was mistaken in his experiment, as he would later be informed that he was. Levi leaves us, at chapter's end, with the wonder that it is the fire of the imagination that can both think of transforming sterile stone into weapons and fuel a prisoner's dream of escape.

A Short History of the Soul

May 13, 2014

It is sunny and blissfully cool in Phoenixville, Pennsylvania. The dog-woods and lilacs are in bloom and the Kentucky coffee trees' purple trumpet flowers already smell sweet. This morning, I was reading Hilton Als's essay 'Triste Tropiques,' an eloquent essay on the strange ways of love, and thinking about composing an essay of my own on a similar theme, when the telephone rang. It was the adoption agency telling me that I have been matched with you, André, a boy from Burundi, two months shy of two years old. Had I known a month ago that I would become your mother, I could have shared this news with my father. He was a good man—my soul's twin, as Als would have it. I already see him in you. If this is wrong, I apologize. But I do.

Last night, 'Take Me To the Water' shook me to the core. James Baldwin's description in this essay of a certain beautiful white man who lost his child to divorce and was adopting another one, black, this time, includes the observation that this man appeared to have emotionally ceased to exist and seemed only to be able to love the helpless. It took me a while to piece together the fact that Baldwin's essay is not just about the emotional poverty of a particular white man. What Baldwin insinuates is that the U.S. is a nation afraid of its own soul.

Baldwin fled New York in 1948 and was living in France when it came to him that he had to return to the States to do his part in freeing blacks from tyranny. 'Take Me To the Water' concludes with a description of the supreme risks Baldwin witnesses in the South taken by those protesting nonviolently. Like Baldwin, my father, who was teaching in Nigeria while reading of the Birmingham riots, knew that he, too, had to return to the States to do what he could.

For a time, my father held the position of the Assistant Director of Council of Human Relations at the Southern Regional Council. He helped secure a grant for the Southwest Alabama Farmer's Cooperative Association to employ people who protested for Civil Rights and had been fired from their workplaces, and he tried (together with the Student Nonviolent Coordinating Committee) to push for economic development that was not capitalist in origin. In fact, it was at a credit union meeting at the Baker County Courthouse in Georgia that my father caught himself thinking that maybe, just maybe, there was a chance that poor whites and poor blacks could work together. This was before a man came up to my father after the meeting to tell him that a white man at the meeting had murdered his brother over a trespassing cow.

One Year Later

What has changed since Baldwin, my father, and so many others risked their lives trying to organize in the South? Today the news repeats itself: a black man is dead and the white man who shot him walks free. At a recent Black Lives Matter protest, I held in my hand a sign that read: *ANGRY.* We remain, on the whole, a profoundly troubled nation.

One year has passed since I received the phone call announcing your presence, one year complete with myriad police killings of black persons, and now your birth country of Burundi is spiraling into chaos at the president's decision to run for a third term. Hundreds of thousands of your countrymen, fearing genocide, have crossed into neighboring countries. In refugee camps, cholera runs rampant.

How is that I came to this point—to the cliff where I dangle perilously, awaiting news of your welfare, hoping beyond hope that I might soon be given the signal that will allow me to travel to adopt you? Maybe our world is too warped to sustain any hope of my becoming your mother. But this is what I know: as my country continues to wage ceaseless, baseless, illegal wars, and your country teeters on the brink of genocide, you are innocent.

August 31, 2015

It is the week following President Nkurunziza's third term inauguration in Bujumbura, Burundi. In the wake of shootings of opposition leaders and their supporters, nuns at your orphanage dress you up in a blue suit and place you in my lap. Your body is rigid. The length of time it takes you to raise your gaze to meet mine feels like years. What it takes for you to look up must, I imagine, require every ounce of strength you have, because the moment our eyes meet, you leave everything you know.

I hold you, my son, dumbfounded.

Acknowledgments

The Bestiality of the Involved was a finalist for the 2019 Pleiades Press Robert C. Jones Award for Short Prose; the 2017 New Rivers Press's Many Voices Project Prose Prize; the 2016 Ohio State University's Nonfiction Collection Prize; the 2015 Sarabande Press's Linda Bruckheimer Series; the 2015 Willow Literature/Aquarius Press prose contest, and the 2014 Autumn House Press' full-length nonfiction contest. The author would like to thank the readers of these contests for their belief in this book. Several essays in this book appeared in journals. 'A Short History of Hostile Soil' (published as 'Hostile Soil') won second place in *Terrain.org*'s 6th annual prose contest November 2015. 'A Short History of Bubbles' (then titled 'Bubbles') won the 2015 *Crab Orchard Review* Special Issue Nonfiction contest and was a Notable Essay in *Best American Essays 2016*. 'The Color of a Poppy' (published as 'A Swath of Poppies') was a finalist for the 2015 TQ6 Open Prose Contest and was published in March 2015 in *Tupelo Quarterly* and nominated for a StorySouth Million Writers Award. 'A Short History of Black Death' (then titled 'Black Death') was published in *Mandala Journal* in 2014. Parts of 'A Short History of Labor' were published as individual poems in *Ladowich*, edited by Jordan Davis and Chris Edgar. 'A Short History of Our Flesh and Blood' appeared in *Southern Indiana Review* and was a Notable Essay in *Best American Essays 2013*. 'A Short History of Reluctant Fundamentalism' (then titled 'Literature in Lahore') won 2nd place in the Nonfiction SLS Unified Literary Awards in 2013, and 'A Short History of the White Gaze' was published (under the title 'The White Gaze') by *Essay Daily* in 2013.

To those at Etruscan Press: thank you for your tireless work on this book. I would also like to thank those whose lives touched mine and who appear—some with names changed to protect their persons—in these pages. In particular, I want to send out shouts to April Freely, friend and reader through thick and thin; my mother Robin Ulmer for her uncompromising and unfaltering belief in me, and my son André Obediah for everything.

ABOUT THE AUTHOR

Spring Ulmer is the author of *Benjamin's Spectacles* and *The Age of Virtual Reproduction*. She teaches at Middlebury College in Vermont.

Books from Etruscan Press

Demonstrategy: Poetry, For and Against | H. L. Hix
First Fire, Then Birds | H. L. Hix
God Bless | H. L. Hix
I'm Here to Learn to Dream in Your Language | H. L. Hix
Incident Light | H. L. Hix
Legible Heavens | H. L. Hix
Lines of Inquiry | H. L. Hix
Rain Inscription | H. L. Hix
Shadows of Houses | H. L. Hix
Wild and Whirling Words: A Poetic Conversation | Moderated by H. L. Hix
All the Difference | Patricia Horvath
Art Into Life | Frederick R. Karl
Free Concert: New and Selected Poems | Milton Kessler
Who's Afraid of Helen of Troy: An Essay on Love | David Lazar
Parallel Lives | Michael Lind
The Burning House | Paul Lisicky
Museum of Stones | Lynn Lurie
Quick Kills | Lynn Lurie
Synergos | Roberto Manzano
The Gambler's Nephew | Jack Matthews
The Subtle Bodies | James McCorkle
An Archaeology of Yearning | Bruce Mills
Arcadia Road: A Trilogy | Thorpe Moeckel
Venison | Thorpe Moeckel
So Late, So Soon | Carol Moldaw
The Widening | Carol Moldaw
Clay and Star: Selected Poems of Liliana Ursu | Translated by Mihaela Moscaliuc
Cannot Stay: Essays on Travel | Kevin Oderman
White Vespa | Kevin Oderman
The Dog Looks Happy Upside Down | Meg Pokrass
Mr. Either/Or | Aaron Poochigian
The Shyster's Daughter | Paula Priamos
Help Wanted: Female | Sara Pritchard
American Amnesiac | Diane Raptosh
Dear Z: The Zygote Epistles | Diane Raptosh
Human Directional | Diane Raptosh
50 Miles | Sheryl St. Germain
Saint Joe's Passion | J.D. Schraffenberger
Lies Will Take You Somewhere | Sheila Schwartz
Fast Animal | Tim Seibles
One Turn Around the Sun | Tim Seibles
Rough Ground | Alix Anne Shaw

A Heaven Wrought of Iron: Poems From the Odyssey | D. M. Spitzer
American Fugue | Alexis Stamatis
Variations in the Key of K | Alex Stein
The Casanova Chronicles | Myrna Stone
Luz Bones | Myrna Stone
In the Cemetery of the Orange Trees | Jeff Talarigo
The White Horse: A Colombian Journey | Diane Thiel
The Arsonist's Song Has Nothing to Do With Fire | Allison Titus
Silk Road | Daneen Wardrop
The Fugitive Self | John Wheatcroft
YOU. | Joseph P. Wood

Etruscan Press Is Proud of Support Received From

Wilkes University

Youngstown State University

The Ohio Arts Council

The Stephen & Jeryl Oristaglio Foundation

The Nathalie & James Andrews Foundation

The National Endowment for the Arts

The New Mexico Community Foundation

Founded in 2001 with a generous grant from the Oristaglio Foundation, Etruscan Press is a nonprofit cooperative of poets and writers working to produce and promote books that nurture the dialogue among genres, achieve a distinctive voice, and reshape the literary and cultural histories of which we are a part.

etruscan press
www.etruscanpress.org

Etruscan Press books may be ordered from

Consortium Book Sales and Distribution
800.283.3572
www.cbsd.com

Etruscan Press is a 501(c)(3) nonprofit organization.
Contributions to Etruscan Press are tax deductible
as allowed under applicable law.
For more information, a prospectus,
or to order one of our titles,
contact us at books@etruscanpress.org.